SKETCHES
for
IMPROVISATION

to
Elizabeth Vanderspar
and
Eric Hollis

SKETCHES
FOR
IMPROVISATION

by

LAURA CAMPBELL

Stainer & Bell, London

© 1986 Laura Campbell
First published in Great Britain by
Stainer & Bell Ltd, 23 Gruneisen Road, London N3 1DZ
Reprinted with corrections, 1997

Companion Volume:
Sketching at the Keyboard (Stainer & Bell, 1982)
ISBN: 0 85249 605 2
ISMN: M 2202 0335 0

Sequel:
Sketches for Further Harmony and Improvisation (Laura Campbell, 1994)
ISBN: 0 9523064 3 3

British Library Cataloguing-in-Publication Data
A catalogue record of this book is available from the British Library

ISBN: 0 85249 652 4
ISMN: M 2202 0334 3

Printed in Great Britain by Galliard (Printers) Ltd, Great Yarmouth

CONTENTS

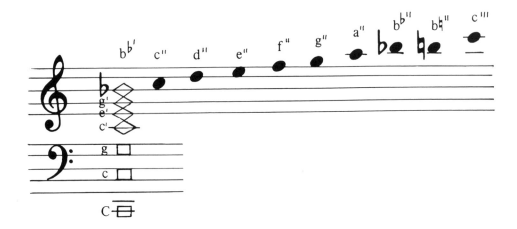

The Harmonic Series with Helmholtz identification

The Author receiving the *Music Teacher* 1983 Music Education Award for *Sketching at the Keyboard*, London May 1983.
Reproduced by permission of the Express and Echo, Exeter.

PREFACE

If keyboard harmonisation of tunes has been considered difficult, hardly within reach of those without an instinctive gift for it, then 'free improvisation' has seemed an even greater challenge. But this is not necessarily so. Improvisation can be easier because you can do what you like: the problem may be to like what you do!

Since the publication of my *Sketching at the Keyboard* (Stainer & Bell, London, 1982) the skill of harmonising given melodies has been proved to be possible for many pianists who had thought they could never master it or whose teachers had not considered encouraging them to try. The course in that book has been followed by child piano pupils, amateur adult pupils, professional music students and class teachers—not solely for examination purposes, but for pure enjoyment.

This book, too, is meant primarily for enjoyment, although it will also be useful for music teachers in school or college, for dance classes and for Dalcroze teachers.

In *Music in the Secondary School Curriculum* (Cambridge University Press, 1982), John Paynter has written:

> We have made important what is examinable,
> instead of making examinable what is important.

As the general standard of keyboard harmony rises, music courses are increasingly encouraging free improvisation—however simple—whether to be examined or not. Simplicity is important, especially at first, because successful improvisation depends on its *effectiveness* from the beginning, not on its technical ease or difficulty. Preoccupation with technique tends to be self-centred rather than music-centred: have the courage to experiment with simple resources.

This 'Sketching' approach encourages solo melodic improvisation in the first place, followed by various harmonic treatments gradually enriching the texture. As every improviser will discover, *any* texture can become monotonous; and the repertory examples show that the masters of composition frequently change from the elaborate to the simple. Learn to do the same and enjoy the changing challenges.

Laura Campbell
Exeter, 1985

HOW TO USE THIS BOOK

This book is based on the same principles as *Sketching at the Keyboard* and is intended to be used alongside it.

The relevant chapters in *Sketching at the Keyboard* are given at the head of each new chapter in this book.

Where *Sketching at the Keyboard* was concerned solely with harmonisation of given melodies, *Sketches for Improvisation* provides material for improvisation on the same processes. Classroom use of the two companion volumes enables teachers of children or adults to keep a mixed ability group working together on the same basic material, through the additional challenge of free improvisation and composition. *Sketches for Improvisation* will be particularly suitable for children in junior departments of conservatoires and music centres, who are expected to produce composition folios from the earliest stages of learning. It will become increasingly useful, too, in schools preparing for the new General Certificate of Secondary Education.

Most exercises in the first seven chapters are within the reach of virtual beginners at the piano, yet extra material is provided throughout to challenge the advanced pianist and the 'instinctive' improviser. Teachers should feel free to vary the order of the different 'Starting Points' according to a pupil's ability, perhaps leaving more difficult technical openings to a later point in the course. Always play the 'Repertory Examples' for careful listening and try to hear recordings of the whole movement or piece.

ACKNOWLEDGEMENT

The extract from 'Calling all Workers' by Eric Coates is reproduced with the permission of International Music Publications.

1 A CONFIDENT START

(*SaK 1*)

Even if you have never tried to improvise before, you will be able to do what is suggested here, as the only basic requirement is that you know the scales of a few simple keys. Natural improvisers, too, may improve their control of phrase structure and variety of texture by working within the given limitations; for without the challenge of some specific plan, many tend to meander formlessly in a favourite style.

If you are a singer, wind or string player, melody will be the most important constituent of your music making. Unfortunately, keyboard players are inclined to undervalue the importance of melody. Making a harmonic accompaniment preoccupies them to the detriment of the melody. Those limited in their training to note-by-note chordal harmonisation of given tunes, played or written, also tend to take melody for granted as 'the thing provided', needing no further consideration. You cannot make music with the attitude 'take a note and put a chord to it'.

Listening to or playing a few works from the classical piano repertory will quickly reveal how often composers use unharmonised melody and that there is nothing inherently inferior about solo melody. Listening to orchestral works, where the forces used are capable of enormous harmonic and textural enrichment, will also demonstrate that melody is a vital element, whatever the instrumentation.

So, if you are a skilled performer with a considerable knowledge of harmony, do not assume that this chapter is too simple for you. It forms the basis of this book's approach to improvisation.

Melody by Ear

Although practical work at the keyboard is essential, it is better to invent your melodies vocally at first (whether actually sung or silently 'auralised') and *then* find out what notes are needed to play them. If you go straight to the keyboard, the temptation is to put down one note after another in the hope that this will produce a tune. But a melody is a *whole* thing and cannot be built note-by-note.

Playing by ear by-passes notation: that is why you are encouraged to

1

think in terms of *ideas* rather than note-names. First, experiment with a well-known tune to see how you can improvise on it without needing to use any chordal knowledge, using the same methods as the classical composers do.

Ex. 1 **Symphony No. 94, 'The Surprise': slow movement**   *Joseph Haydn*

Degrees: 1   3   5   3   4   2   7   5

[Repeat of first phrase]   8   4♯   5

                                                     [7   8 in new key]

(i)   Play the melody.

(ii)   Close your eyes and sing it from memory.

(iii) Play it from memory. When you play by ear like this, ask yourself, 'What degree of the scale is each melody note?'. The numbers below the melody in this example show these degrees; unlike note names, they will *stay the same in any key*. Tonic solfa syllables may be equally helpful at first.

(iv)   The melody has ended in a new key and is now 'at home' in the key of G. Play it again, this time starting in G. Think of the degree numbers in the new scale, *not* the notes by name.

Melody and Variation

You could now repeat example 1 in many keys. A melody repeated without change may be acceptable in a song, where the words are different in each verse. But when musicians began to improvise longer pieces of solo instrumental music they needed to find substitutes for verbal variation to sustain interest. The answer lay in making musical 'variations'. The earliest and simplest variations were what composers in the 17th and 18th centuries called 'Divisions' or 'Doubles'. These were repetitions of a melody, ornamented by smaller, faster-moving note divisions. With Haydn's melody as a theme, the process of variation by Divisions or Doubles can easily be put into practice like this:

2

(i) Play the melody in the key of G as a sturdy march, reduced to ♩ values by cutting out the repeated notes. Give it strength and drive by *doubling the melody an octave below* with your left hand. Play with a stately legato touch.

(ii) Extend the material by repeating the theme in the key of degree number '5', D, at which you have now arrived. Start on *d'* with the right hand and you will end on *a'*, next to the *g'* on which the theme began: this leads neatly into a repeat in the original key of G.

(iii) Music originates within man, not just as a thinker but as *a musical instrument himself*. As the voice was the instigator of song, so the body, in simple dance movements, took the lead as instigator of instrumental rhythmic variations. Change the speed and character of this piece from marching to running, by dividing each ♩ into two ♪, played by alternate right and left hands. Use 3rd fingers only throughout (thumb and other fingers relaxed alongside) with a sharp staccato touch as one hand gets out of the way of the other. Play the first ♪ with the right hand and the repetition with the left, using a hand touch working from the wrist, right hand *over* left. Your hands imitate running feet and you should practise first on the closed lid of the piano to get the right touch. After you reach the new key at the end of the theme, return to the original key by *undoing* the raised degree '4', like this:

Ex. 2

Degree: 1   3   5   4♮   3   2

(iv) Repeat the piece in G again, this time playing it in a skipping rhythm which may be either ♩♪ or ♩.♪ . Repeat the figure twice to each melody note. Start with the *left* hand, again staccato:

Ex. 3

Notice that this time in the final bar the right hand has been left behind on degree '5' of the scale to form a reiterated 'pivot note' alternating with the melodic notes of this link bar.

3

You will also notice that despite the quickening of decorative notes, the pace of the original theme has now been halved to ♩ for each change of melody note.

(v)   Keeping this pace for the melody, octaves may be used in another way. For this variation it might seem suitable to change from G major to G minor:

Ex. 4

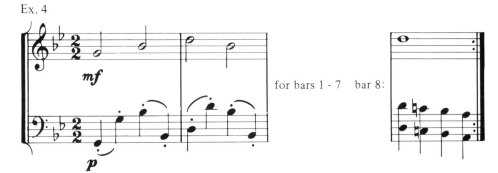

for bars 1 - 7   bar 8:

(vi)   Play the whole sequence from memory, based on note 'divisions' ♩, ♫, ♩. ♪ and ♩. If you can hear or study a score of the whole slow movement, you will find that Haydn uses all the methods of variation with which you are now familiar: octave doubling at several registers (bar 49), doubling of melody-note divisions by reiterating the same note (bar 75) conversion to a dotted skip rhythm (bar 115) ... and the theme transferred into the tonic minor key (bar 49 again).

Repertory Examples

Here is more evidence that composers employ precisely the techniques which you can now use in improvisation.

Ex. 5 Concerto for Harpsichord (BWV 1052): opening   *J. S. Bach*

4

This is a simple example of the strength of octave doubling. Later in the movement come extended passages based on the device of alternating hands, which you used in variations (iii) and (iv) on the Haydn theme. Here Bach keeps the right hand on one pivot note instead of repeating the same note with each hand. Such alternate-hand playing was easier on harpsichords with two manuals than it may be on the piano:

Ex. 6   Concerto for Harpsichord (BWV 1052): first movement, bars 62 - 64   *J. S. Bach*

Here is an example with a fuller texture:

Ex. 7   Le Tic-Toc-Choc or Les Maillotins ('Pièce Croisée'): opening   *F. Couperin*

*Couperin suggested that, if you had only one manual, the left hand should be played an octave lower. On the piano it is better to raise the register of the right hand part.

Later French composers, such as Ravel in the *Sonatine* and Debussy in *Jardins sous la pluie* adapted the same technique in simple or enriched form. Spanish composers have used it to imitate the repeated notes which are a feature of much guitar music, as in:

Ex. 8   Seguidillas, op. 232 no. 5: bars 5 - 8   *I. Albeniz*

The alternating octave texture of variation (v) on the Haydn theme occurs in Bach, like this:

Ex. 9   Concerto for Harpsichord (BWV 1052): first movement, bars 28 - 30   *J. S. Bach*

and

5

Melody Making

You can now make use of these processes to improvise your own melodies and make variations on them. But no amount of dressing up can redeem a dull melody. Here are some common misconceptions and errors in melody-making:

(a)   The belief that each melody *note* should be different from the previous one is discouraging in that it makes the task more onerous than it need be, as it keeps you wondering 'What note shall I play next?'. Many good melodies include repetition of notes of the same pitch:

Ex. 11   Double Concerto for Violin and Cello, op. 102: third movement, opening   *J. Brahms*

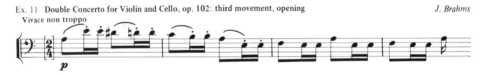

(Brahms treats this theme by octave doubling, at several registers.)

(b)   The belief that each *phrase* should be different from the previous phrase is discouraging, in that it leads you to think that you need to create more material than is either necessary or musically advisable. Melody making is greatly simplified when you realise how much you can do with a single short phrase, repeated and then developed in simple ways:

Ex. 12   Aria from the cantata 'Also hat Gott die Welt geliebt' (BWV 68)   *J. S. Bach*

Notice that Bach repeats the first phrase identically. He then develops the rhythmic pattern of the first two beats at a higher pitch, giving an apex to the total melody. This leaves space for a considerable descent to bring the phrase to a resting point. So the whole melody winds up and then winds down, all in a shapely fashion.

An easy and effective way to build a four-phrase melody out of a single phrase is:

(i) Think of a phrase in the key of G, or use this:

Ex. 13

(ii) Repeat the same phrase in the Dominant key (key of the 5th degree).
(iii) Repeat the phrase in the original key.
(iv) Invent a final balancing phrase, which either descends or ascends to the keynote.

The suggested phrase—or one of your own—could then be further developed like this:

(v) Repeat the original phrase.
(vi) Repeat it in the key of the 2nd degree of the scale (A minor).
(vii) Repeat it by rising to the relative minor key, that of the 6th degree (E minor).
(viii) Start your final phrase by cancelling the recent *d♯'*, which will lead easily into a final phrase in the home key. If the last phrase of your first section rose to the high keynote, *g''*, it could drop to the lower *g'* this time, or *vice versa*.

You have now produced a sixteen-bar melody out of a single two-bar phrase. That phrase must be a musical unit of sufficient character to be easily memorised. Notice how the three repeats in the second section inevitably make a crescendo and build up a purposeful climax. See if you can repeat the whole by memory. You will find that you scarcely need to think of individual notes, only the *ideas* which governed the placing of each new phrase.

(c) A poor melody which is dull—and therefore difficult to memorise and repeat—may result from the player becoming bogged down in one area of the key, reminiscent of a dog pottering round in a kennel, instead of someone striding over a great open space. The weakest hymn tunes tend to be in this category. The best way to free yourself from this error is to start with a common chord in arpeggio:

Ex. 14   Brandenburg Concerto No. 5 (BWV 1050): opening   *J. S. Bach*

(d)   The opposite error, that of excessive leaping around, produces a disjointed, awkward and purposeless line of pitches, again difficult to memorise. Most good melodies involve a pleasing combination of leaps and stepwise movement:

Ex. 15   March 'Calling All Workers'   *Eric Coates*

Notice the repetition of the stepwise first bar as bar 3, while the second bar is developed by a rise in pitch in bar 4. No melody strides more joyfully forwards than this one, with the subsequent propulsion up the common chord providing an apex in the third quarter followed by a scalic descent, which rises on the final note to maintain the drive into the continuation.

(e)   A four-sectioned melody which sits down on the keynote at the end of the third section tends to fall flat. The piece will seem to terminate prematurely and a further phrase seem redundant. A positive answer to the question, 'Was your journey really necessary?' depends upon the third quarter convincing the listener that an interesting musical voyage has been made, from which the final phrase returns home. In a simple melody, such as that used in ex. 13 where the third phrase (because it repeats the first) does end on the keynote, this may seem acceptable. But any sense of premature termination may be avoided in this and other melodies by ending on a note other than the keynote. In the case of Ex. 13, the third phrase might end on the 2nd or 4th degree:

Ex. 16
[Phrase 3]

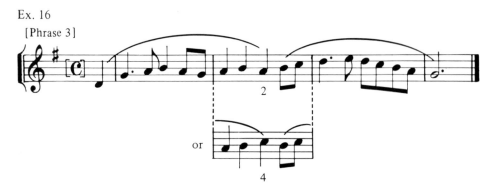

8

Finally it should be said that if the invention of melodies comes easily to you it is not necessary to think consciously of these points of detail, but better to work spontaneously. Subsequent examination of a melody may then reveal that you have done such things naturally. But for many people, even trained musicians, melody-making is a weak area, probably because it has been assumed to be easy and given little attention.

Starting Points

Now apply what you have learnt to making your own melodies.

(i) Make a well structured melody beginning like this:

Ex. 17

Degree: 1   3   5   8

Then make a variation on your completed tune by the alternating hands device, playing each melody note twice.

(ii) Combine these leaps with predominantly stepwise movements:

Ex. 18

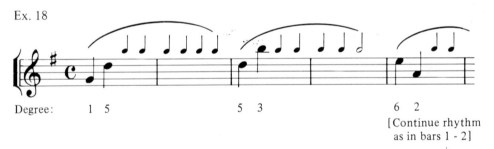

Degree: 1 5   5   3   6   2

[Continue rhythm as in bars 1 - 2]

Repeat your tune with each note played twice in a skip rhythm, in simple or compound time (♩. ♪ or ♩ ♪).

(iii) Most melodies are made up of notes of varying length, but it is also possible to make a melody with almost continuous notes of equal length at a running *or* walking pace.

Ex. 19 Symphony No. 9 in D: the 'Ode to Joy' theme   *L. van Beethoven*

This is a famous example of an equal-note melody. If you know it, play the whole tune from memory; if you do not, improvise a continuation.

9

Then double it at the octave as a March (which Beethoven does). Realise that even a texture of continuous equal-length notes must still have a clear phrase structure or it will not make sense. If a phrase implies termination on a long note, the end of that phrase can nevertheless be linked to the next by a 'fill-in' of some kind, like this:

Ex. 20

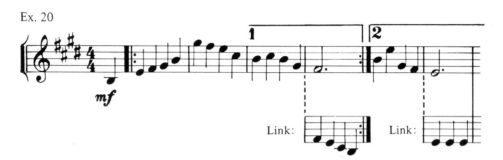

(The last bar could move up a degree and back or *vice versa*.)

Here are further openings:

(iv)

Ex. 21

(v)

Ex. 22

(vi)

Ex. 23

(vii)

Ex. 24

Treat this as a funeral march, doubling it with the left hand *two* octaves below throughout your improvisation.

(viii)

Ex. 25

Do not slip into $\frac{6}{4}$ time without realising it. Five-time rhythms tend to swing along in either a $2 + 3$ or $3 + 2$ grouping. Here is a $3 + 2$ theme. Feel it as a skip followed by two runs:

Ex. 26

(ix)

Ex. 27

(x)

Ex. 28

(xi)

Ex. 29

p *legato cantabile*

(The rhythmic grouping here is 2 + 3 + 2.)

(xii) There is a natural tendency at the keyboard to start a melody on the keynote of your chosen key; but if you first invent your themes in your head you will find that they start on various degrees of the scale and so produce more varied tunes. Notice the degrees on which the starting points above have begun. Experiment in starting your own melodies, one on each degree of the scale.

(xiii) Here is a suggestion for improvising a piece using the 5th-degree pivot note as an accompanimental texture alternating with the notes of the melody *below* it. Play the left-hand melody with a singing legato touch:

Ex. 30

Key A minor

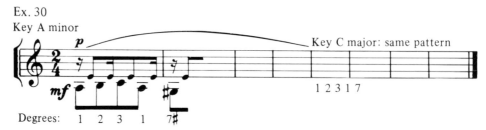

Key C major: same pattern

1 2 3 1 7

Degrees: 1 2 3 1 7♯

Invent some melodies using this process in major and minor keys, with the melody above or below the pivot note.

(xiv) Using this opening, continue with the octave accompaniment in alternating registers and experiment with changing over parts as in bar 3.

Ex. 31

Key C minor

12

Folios

It is a good plan to write out a few of your improvisations and start a folio of pieces which have particularly pleased you. Such a collection will provide encouraging evidence of your progress: some pieces may be improved by further work; others may be worth keeping as themes to develop later. Many composers keep 'sketch-books' of ideas to use in later compositions, perhaps turning a song tune into a chamber movement (*cf.* Schubert in the 'Trout' Quintet), or a solo piece into a concerto movement (*cf.* Schumann in the A minor Piano Concerto)—so you will be in good company! Hence the importance of melodic invention, which may start as a humble idea improvised at the piano and end up one day in an extended work.

2 COUNTERPOINT OUT OF UNISON

(SaK 1)

Music, to be music at all, must move along horizontally in the time dimension. As the eye follows a line in a drawing, so the ear follows a line of music. This line consists of a progression of sounds which, like a sentence in speech, *makes sense*. A word by itself, or a single note, single interval or single chord is meaningless. It is only in the relationship of one such to another *in a context* that strokes on a drawing or spots on a pointillist painting are 'blended by the eye' as the dictionary says, or that musical sounds are linked together by the ear to make sense. Where improvisation at the keyboard is concerned, the note-by-note approach is too slow a process of thought to enable the music to move. It is not only more musical but also much easier to think in terms of musical *units*, each comprising a group of sounds which can be treated as a single idea.

Variations on a Motif

The first chapter emphasised the importance of repetition in music. A repeated phrase starting on a different degree of the scale, or in a different key, is known as a sequence. Sequence is a very important element of musical structure and you can make good use of it in improvisation.

(i)   Play the first three notes of the scale of C as your melodic unit, then develop it in ascending sequence to the top of the scale:

Ex. 32

(ii)   Invert this 3-note motif, mirror-fashion: then put it up an octave. Treat this version sequentially, so that both motif and progression descend, beginning:

Ex. 33

(iii)   Play the two-bar ascending sequence followed by the descending sequence, doubled by the left hand an octave below.

(iv)   Play the ascending motif once only from *c′* with the right hand and immediately repeat it in the inverted direction so that you have a six-note pattern composed of the motif with its inversion. The shape of the pattern is ⋀ . Invert the pattern with the left hand, making the shape ⋁ . Then combine the two: ◇ .

(v)   This now forms a two-part unit from the original motif. Repeat it sequentially, ascending the scale. Then exchange parts, the pattern becoming ✕ and play in descending sequence. Exchanging parts like this forms the basis of what is sometimes called 'invertible counterpoint'.

(vi)   Return to the original 3-note ascending motif with the right hand and accompany it with its own inversion in the left hand: ⟨ . Develop this shorter two-part unit in ascending sequence. Reverse the parts to descend, right hand as Ex. 33. It is important still to *think in terms of parallel octave doubling* of the 3-note motif and, at the same time *visualise* the left-hand notes mirror-wise. To be sure you can do this, put down all three notes simultaneously with both hands, in what is called a 'note-cluster'. Repeat with the next ascending cluster:

Ex. 34

Rhythmic Variations

Many a horizontally running stretch of music may be spun out of a single idea in this way. Play the contrapuntal motif of (vi) above in the following rhythms. Remember that each allows four alternatives, as there are two choices of direction for the motif itself and two choices for the direction of the sequence. Exchanging the different upper and lower

15

rhythms now adds further possibilities. Use the keys of C, F, G or D and in each case, reverse right and left hand rhythms on descending the scale:

(i)

Ex. 35

 (*i.e.* omit the middle note in one hand)

(ii)

Ex. 36

(iii)

Ex. 37

To practise this cross-rhythm, realise that the left hand is the same as in (ii) above, while the right hand is as (ii) with the last two notes tied:

Ex. 38

(iv) Convert the 3-note motif into a 4-note one by returning to the first note in one hand, while the other moves at half the speed by omission of the middle note:

Ex. 39 Tempo ♪ = walk, ♪ = run.

(v)

Ex. 40

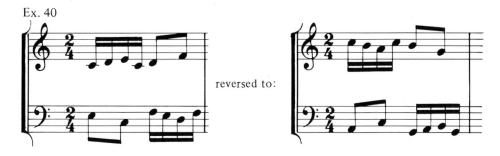

reversed to:

(vi) Experiment to discover how many different rhythmic patterns you can find. Remember it is possible to repeat some notes, also to use groupings of five sub-divisions.

Adding 'Hot Cross Buns' Bass

By mixing the various units you have been practising you can now make attractive short pieces, adding the 'HXB' bass for phrase endings (*SaK* pp. 20–21):

(i) (a) In $\frac{4}{4}$ time, use the 4-over-2 note pattern of Ex. 39 three times in ascending sequence, returning on the fourth beat to the d'-e'-f' unit. Repeat the first two units; then run home down the scale from 5th to 1st degree over HXB. This two-bar phrase forms the first section of your piece, to be extended by sequential development as follows:

(b) Imitate the whole of (a) sequentially, starting the melody on the 5th degree. (You will be using the g'-a'-b' cluster and putting the phrase into the key of G.) As your left hand ended (a) on bass clef c, start this section with neighbouring B in that hand for a smooth link, using registration two octaves apart.

(c) Repeat (a) in the key of the 3rd degree, returning to one octave registration.

(d) Play the 4-over-2 motif in C as in Ex. 39 and repeat it in sequence all the way up the scale, changing the bass to HXB on the last two beats.

17

(e)   Replay the whole piece (a) to (d), making eight bars. Notice
       how the uninterrupted ascent in the final section gives shape
       and climax to the whole piece. When this extended scalic
       sequence was used alone it became a monotonous exercise,
       but used at an appropriate place it can relieve monotony:
       'where' is so often just as important as 'what'.

(ii)   Using the same initial two-bar phrase, develop it in the following
       set of keys:

       (a)   key C.
       (b)   key of the 4th degree (F), with two-octave registration.
       (c)   key of the 2nd degree (D minor).
       (d)   build the climax as in (i) (d) but start with the cluster *a-b-c'*.
              Ascend in sequence for six beats and use the last two beats to
              re-establish the key of C, with the neighbouring right-hand
              cluster over **HXB**.

   One of the reasons why so many students and even professional
musicians feel diffident about trying to improvise is that, having been
taught harmony in terms of chords in single lumps, they feel unable to
think of enough *new material*, enough 'different chords' to make a whole
piece. Most music *is* composed from a surprisingly small vocabulary of
chords. To improvise, it is much more important to use a variety of keys
than a wide variety of close textured chords. A key is a chord expanded:
a chord is a key reduced. The important difference is that while a single
chord means nothing, an area of music *however simple* in a single key
may have plenty to say. You have made the last two pieces without
needing any chords, but using keys in (i) on degrees 1, 5, 3 and 1, and in
version (ii) keys on degrees 1, 4, 2 and 1.

(iii) Here is a more elaborate initial phrase which can be similarly
       treated:

Ex. 41

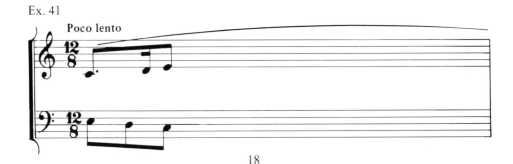

18

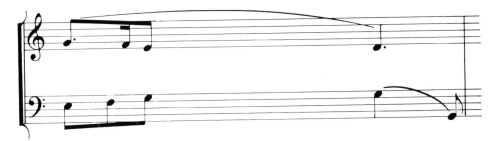

(a) Play the motif four times in ascending sequence; then think of the 3-note cluster below the one you have last used, and invert that in each hand (reverse of first-beat pattern). Use this in descending sequence for three beats, coming to a stop on the fourth beat to make a phrase ending which indicates continuation, as it does not end on the keynote.

(b) Repeat the phrase in the key on the 5th degree (G) with appropriate registration.

(c) Drop the right hand to begin the motif on *a* and repeat in that key.

(d) Invent your own final two bars.

(iv) Use or adapt these frameworks to make short pieces on any of the rhythmic patterns previously suggested.

Contrary Motion

Harmony and counterpoint are too often thought of as two distinct subjects, which is a great mistake. Most good counterpoint of the last 400 years has a sound harmonic basis and most good harmony—like a well-built house—has a vertical structure *and* horizontal lines which proceed with a sense of their own. This well-known quotation illustrates both aspects:

Ex. 42 Minuet (BWV Anh. 114), bars 9 - 16   *J. S. Bach*

The harmonic structure of the bass may be regarded as unravelled into a contrapuntal line, partnering the treble line.

Now compare the effect of treating the 3-note motif in mirror image inversion and by contrary motion *from the same starting note*:

Ex. 43

(a)

(b)

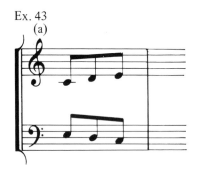 

You will have heard that treatment (b) totally alters the harmonic character, changing the harmony from major to minor. In moving freely in contrary motion, as opposed to thinking mirror-wise, it is harder to anticipate what the combined effect will be and what it may lead on to. But there are ways in which freer contrary motion can also be used in terms of a single idea. Extend your contrapuntal vocabulary with the single idea 'scale' like this:

(i)   Play the scale of C, one octave up and down, doubled at the octave by the left hand, in *similar* motion.

(ii)   Play *one* octave up and down with the left hand, but this time play the right hand scale twice as fast as the left, so it will cover *two* octaves up and down.

(iii)   Play the same on the white-note scale starting on *A* and *a*.

(iv)   Start the scale of C with the hands *two* octaves apart. Play the bass scale twice as fast as the treble scale. Repeat on the A minor scale.

(v)   Start with *both* thumbs on *c'* and play the same scale in *contrary motion*, first with the right hand twice as fast as the left, then vice versa. Repeat from *a*.

(vi)   Start the scale with the hands one octave apart. Ascend one octave with the left hand while the right, moving twice as fast, covers one octave up *and* down. You will change from similar to contrary motion mid-way. Repeat on the scale of G major, then on the scale of D minor (with flattened 6th degree or not, as you wish, but *not* a raised 7th degree). In all these combined scales the mixture of concordant and dissonant intervals proves acceptable because either the notes which coincide are concordant or the ensuing passing-note brings a concordant resolution,

20

and the two concurrent melodic *lines* carry conviction. You can use this process in any rhythm and stop at virtually any point to make a phrase ending, in the same or a related key:

Ex. 44a

Experiment with each of these examples, reaching the same key by making the opposite hand go faster. Sometimes make a new phrase-ending in a different related key. Sometimes change the bar time and the rhythmic patterns.

Here are two more frameworks to show you how you can use these *ideas* of sequence, inversion, contrary motion, and doubling and halving speeds to improvise more varied pieces:

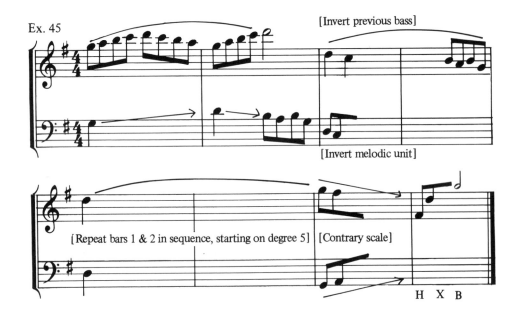

Ex. 45

[Invert previous bass]

[Invert melodic unit]

[Repeat bars 1 & 2 in sequence, starting on degree 5] [Contrary scale]

H X B

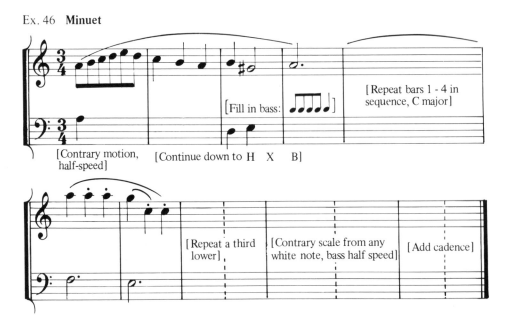

Ex. 46 **Minuet**

[Fill in bass: ♩♩♩♩♩]

[Repeat bars 1 - 4 in sequence, C major]

[Contrary motion, half-speed]   [Continue down to H X   B]

[Repeat a third lower]

[Contrary scale from any white note, bass half speed]

[Add cadence]

Replay from memory, thinking of the constructional processes you are using.

Combining Mobile and Static

Another easy use of the mobile scale is to combine it with its opposite, a long sound of static pitch.

(i)   Play, with the left hand, one octave *down and up* of the scale of C, started on its 5th degree, *g*. Accompany this with right-hand repeated notes remaining on the 5th degree, one *g'* to each degree of the bass scale. Repeat, the left-hand scale descending from *c'* beneath right-hand repeated notes on *c"*.

(ii)   Reverse the process, the right hand playing the scale *up and down* from *c'* over repeated left-hand Cs (starting two octaves apart). Repeat with each hand starting on the 5th degree (*g'* and *G* respectively).

(iii)   Repeat the scale from *G* to *g* in the bass, but this time *trill* the right-hand part, ornamenting the repeated *g'* with the note above:

Ex. 47

Quicken the right hand to a triplet at the end of the trill so that both hands end on a G.

(iv)   Play similar trills in the bass under treble scales, starting in either direction. Such trills were often used in harpsichord music to sustain a single long sound above or below a mobile passage. Before the development of the modern piano it was impossible for a note struck once to last more than an instant, and even on the piano a note will inevitably fade after the hammer has struck; but by using repeated notes or trills a *crescendo* in the mobile part can be matched by a *crescendo* in the part of static pitch. Notice again how much more music can be produced by the use of ideas with a single source than by working note-by-note.

A Set of Variations

Using all the processes shown so far, you should now be able to improvise a set of variations on the folk song 'Down in Demerara' (*SaK*, p. 22). Memorise the melody.

(i)   Play the melody solo.

(ii)   Double it at the octave.

(iii) Alternate right-hand and left-hand third fingers in a running tempo, repeating each ♩ as ♪♩ with a marked staccato touch.

(iv)   Play a similar variation, but with each left-hand off-beat ⁷♪ on the 5th degree pivot-note, *d'*, throughout (except where the half beat is present in the melody). Fill out the final bar with ♪♪♪♪ ♩ alternating lower degrees of the tonic chord with the pivot-note.

(v)   Repeat (iv) with the melody in the tonic *minor* key. Which is the only note you need alter?

(vi)   Increase the divisions while slackening the pace to a more lyrical movement, playing in triplets with two left-hand pivot-notes:

Ex. 48

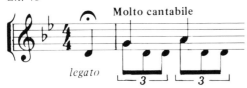

(vii) Return to G major with a lively variation in which the left hand plays the melody beneath a right-hand pivot-note repeated on the off-beat. Or use a trill on the 5th degree instead of the pivot-note, in divisions 2 to 1 or 4 to 1 of the melodic beat, a choice which will affect the speed of the melody. End as you think fit.

(viii) Make a variation in two-part counterpoint by inverting the melody in the bass. The unit for inversion will be the first **five** notes of the scale. Start the left hand on *d* and leap up an octave into the first bar of inversion. Remember that when the right hand moves up the left hand moves down, and vice versa. Is inversion satisfactory right to the end? If not, make any adaptation you prefer.

(ix)   Play (vii) and (viii) in the tonic minor key.

(x)   As a strong *finale*, replay the major version in invertible counterpoint (vii) with each hand doubled at the octave and widely spaced registration between the two hands.

Starting Points

(i)

Ex. 49

Remember HXB can reverse its direction, as can scales or any other unit.

(ii)

Ex. 50

Accompany this solely with HXB in changing registers. In bar 2 develop the rhythmic pattern of bar 1 (first *or* second half). As the piece progresses use other keys, but end in the original key.

(iii)

Ex. 51

Modulate to the key of degree '5' (G) in bar 4. Start a second section in that key, using a descending bass scale in its third bar; or invert the unit in this section and treat it in descending sequence twice or more, perhaps to end in E minor. Continue as you wish and end in the original key.

25

(iv)

Ex. 52

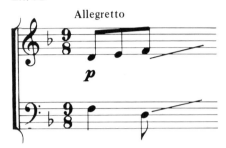

Exchange the rhythms where you wish.

(v)

Ex. 53

This is a two-beat *rhythmic* unit derived from the one-beat *melodic* motif in (iv) above. Try similar adaptations, such as  or *vice versa* or *vice versa*, in various keys, major or minor.

(vi)

Ex. 54

(vii)

Ex. 55

(viii)

Ex. 56

This treble motif has a passing note above as well as between the mirror exchange of the two bass notes. As another improvisation, change the rhythmic grouping from 2 + 3 to 3 + 2:

Ex. 57

Note the *a'* appoggiatura in this second version and compare it with the Bach Minuet of Ex. 42, bar 6.

(ix)

Ex. 58

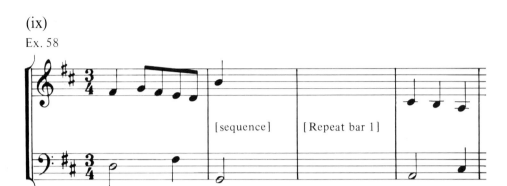

[sequence]   [Repeat bar 1]

This opening is bar 6 of Ex. 42 in the key of D. Increase its expressiveness by adding an appoggiatura in the fourth bar of your improvisation like this:

Ex. 59

(x)

Ex. 60

Dolce

mf

[sequence up] [inversion of bar 1]

[repeat bars 1 - 2 with bass 8ve lower]

Continue with your own middle section, which could reach a climax by rising to f'' in the melody. Then repeat the first section, in which you could start with the lower registration in the left hand. Then return to the former register of bar 4 by rising from the tied c.

(xi)

Ex. 61

Bar 2 will follow naturally in sequence one degree lower; try the first left-hand note as g and then as $g^\sharp$. Choose which you prefer and complete your improvisation.

(xii)

Ex. 62

Folio

Add some of these improvisations to your written folio, improving or extending them if you wish, by further work at the piano.

3 ONE-CHORD IMPROVISATION

(*SaK 2*)

Though this chapter involves different activities for right and left hands, it allows again for prime concentration on melodic invention as the left hand needs no separate thought.

(i)   Play:

Ex. 63

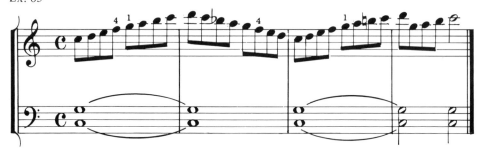

Retaining the same relationship of registration, play both parts an octave lower.

(ii)   Treat the bass of the same example as though it were a drum rhythm, playing left-hand 5ths softly and crisply with a wrist staccato touch. For this exercise use only the natural *b'* in the right hand:

Ex. 64

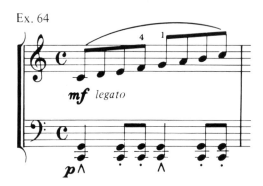

(iii) In the previous chapter, passing notes were used to link two notes a third apart. Another kind of passing note involves alternation between the note on a beat with the note immediately above or below it. This ornamental principle is known as a *mordent*—an *upper mordent* or *lower mordent*, according to its direction. The pattern may be played slowly or quickly, *legato* or *staccato*, and in various rhythmic patterns. Play the scale of F ascending, ornamenting each degree with a lower mordent:

Ex. 65

Then play the descending scale using *upper* mordents.

(iv) Improvise a melody over tonic 5ths beginning with the F major scale, ornamented with upper or lower mordents, or progressing by scalic passing notes. During phrase endings on long notes keep the left hand always on the tonic 5th in the same rhythm, until the final note of the piece. Playing a 'drone' bass like this should soon become automatic, forming a soft background above which you can concentrate on your melodic invention. If you have any difficulty with this, *sing* an improvised melody over the left-hand 5ths to begin with.

Starting Points

In each piece play 2–4 bars of bass rhythm as an 'Introduction' before bringing in your melody, as in (i). If you still find it hard to co-ordinate left and right hand, first play your melody and tap the accompanying rhythm with the flat of your left hand on your left thigh. When you play the 5ths an appropriate touch is essential; sometimes a light vivacious bass will support a smooth melody: sometimes a smooth bass may be more suitable.

(i)

Ex. 66

(a) Use only the ♩ rhythm in the melody to start with, improvising 8–16 bars.

(b) Include different note lengths on the lines suggested in the example. Try to remember your first eight bars so that you can repeat them to end the piece.

(ii)

Ex. 67

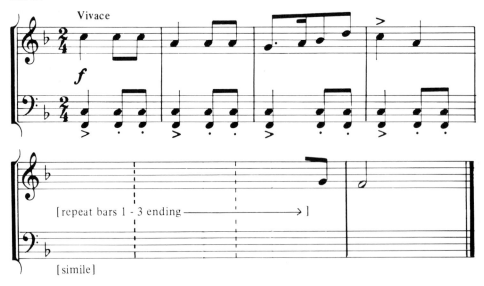

32

Follow these bars by a two-bar phrase, with a melody in the rhythm
♩. ♫♫ | ♫ ♩ ♩, repeated with a change of register.

(iii)

Ex. 68

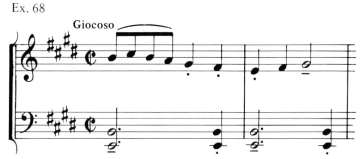

Continue over the same rhythm, making sequential use of bar 2.

(iv)

Ex. 69

(v)   One of the easy things about using bass 5ths is that, except for the two perfect 5ths above B flat and B natural, all the others are either two white or two black notes. Try them all with your left hand, ascending chromatically from C. Playing a 5ths accompaniment in keys with many sharps or flats is no more difficult than playing in C major. A *cantabile* melody often sounds particularly lovely in 'black-note keys', as the Romantic composers so often found. Whether you think of this opening as in the key of C sharp or D flat does not matter: just correct a melody note if it does not sound as you intended:

Ex. 70

(vi)

Ex. 71

Follow a first eight-bar section (two eight-beat phrases) with a middle section of similar length in a lower register. Start the melody in this middle section on the same *d″* but *descend* the chord. Recapitulate the first section.

(vii)

Ex. 72

Remember that mordents can travel in either direction, and by whole or half tones.

(viii)

Ex. 73

This close registration of melody and bass often suits an improvisation in a low register.

(ix)   Lift the left hand well off the ♪ at the end of the pattern or you may find yourself adding another 5th at the end of the bar:

Ex. 74

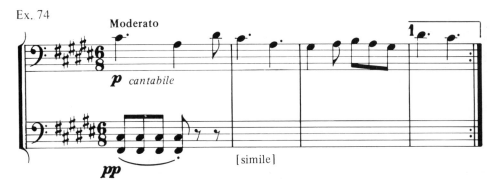

Invent another melody in F sharp major over the same bass.

(x)

Ex. 75   **Rumba**

(a)   Notation here looks much more complicated than it sounds. In preparing to play your introductory bars of rhythm count '123,456,78' in ♪ s. This common rumba rhythm consists of two compound beats and one simple beat. Do not practise it too fast until the left hand can continue automatically without your thinking of the division of the beats.

(b)   Play the first two bars repeatedly, with both hands as an accompaniment, then sing a melody over them, beginning:

Ex. 76

Accompaniment:

(xi)

Ex. 77   Tango

If you wish, add other chromatic semitones as you continue, so long as the basic structure of your melody maintains the key. Make a middle section in C major *or* C minor.

(xii)

Ex. 78

Steady

Repertory Examples

Ex. 79   L'Arlésienne Suite No. 2: Farandole, bars 5 - 8   *G. Bizet*

36

Ex. 80   Tambourin

J-P. Rameau

Ex. 81   L'Arlesienne Suite No. 2, Carillon: opening

G. Bizet

[Bells throughout]

Ex. 82   Casse Noisette: Danse Arabe, bars 5 - 8

P. I.Tschaikowsky

37

Linking with Counterpoint

Improvise a complete piece in ternary form (A—B—A) using the processes studied in this and the previous chapter:

Section A^1 in two-part counterpoint

Section B   a contrasting section, of melody over tonic bass 5th rhythmic pattern

Section A^2 repetition of the first section, perhaps with a short coda

In addition to these main contrasts of *texture* between the sections, you can vary *keys*—major or minor—and *time signatures*, using simple or compound time. The completed piece should make a convincing whole: whether it is simple or elaborate is not important.

Folio

Maintain a record of your progress through these first three chapters, to include a piece in ternary form, as above.

4 TWO-CHORD IMPROVISATION

(*SaK 3,9*)

Chords I and V[7] were the linchpin in music of the Haydn, Mozart and Beethoven period. This is not to say that they did not use other chords; but clear tonality and form in their music were established and kept in control by these two basic chords, often reiterated at the end of long movements like a piece clapping itself. Analysis reveals that they are also vital to the whole structure. One of the wittiest pieces ever written is based almost entirely on these chords. You do not have to play the piece as Beethoven wrote it to appreciate the jokes, for you can hear them simply by playing landscaping 5ths under the melody—which makes it easy to play up to speed:

Ex. 83   Bagatelle, op. 33 no. 3: opening   *L. van Beethoven*

You surely relished the surprise of the harmonies of Tonic and Dominant bouncing up to such an unexpected key in bar 5. Notice how Beethoven teases on the 5th degree of the scale being common to both chords I and V, as he ties those leaping octave Cs over the changing chords beneath.

Starting Points

Remember the advice on pages 6–12 on improvising good tunes which *flow* melodically and rhythmically. You are unlikely to make enjoyable melodies by thinking theoretically of the notes which make up the two triads you are going to use, such as:

Ex. 84

Although Haydn's tune of example 1 does in fact go up and down the arpeggios of I and V^7, he will have thought of it aurally *as* a melody. In each of these starting points, first *sing* a melody while you play the left-hand 5ths, then play what you have just sung. Start these different improvisations from each note of the tonic or dominant chord, as shown, and sing a spontaneous melody which flows from that single note. Explore the possibilities fully by descending from that note or ascending from it. (*Never* include the 3rd of the chord within the left-hand 5ths, a habit which, once developed, is difficult to eradicate (see *SaK*, p. 42).)

(i)   Use the same bass under every four-bar phrase:

Ex. 85
(a)

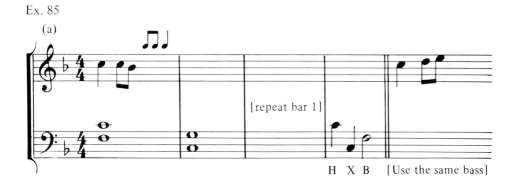

(b)

(c)

(ii) Use the same bass under each of these beginnings, varying the register:

Ex. 86

[repeat bar 1]

I

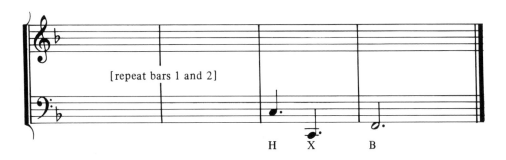

[repeat bars 1 and 2]

H   X   B

Ex. 87

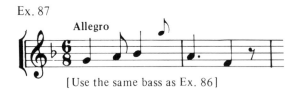

[Use the same bass as Ex. 86]

Ex. 88

molto leggiero

As the harmony of this opening changes within the bar, you may like to use the bass framework twice under eight bars of melody.

Ex. 89

Try starting on each harmony note of either chord for new improvisations in which you can also exchange the time signatures and try others. There are so many possibilities that no one should *ever* ask, 'How can I possibly improvise with a vocabulary of only two chords?'. Folk musicians in many countries and in many ages have done so.

Using Related Keys

Improvisation is largely a matter of re-creating familiar sounds and hand patterns which have become familiar through aural and manual memory. Play this phrase with tonic 5th underneath the first bar and HXB under the second. (Notice that the left-hand thumb is already on the 5th degree of the scale for 'Hot'.)

Ex. 90

Now extend your range of keys by playing the phrase in these related keys:

Tonic (C major)
Dominant (G major)
Key on the 3rd degree (E minor)
Key on the 6th degree (A minor)
Key on the 2nd degree (D minor)
Key on the 4th degree (F major)
returning to
Tonic (C major)

Make up a melody of your own over the same bass and play it in the same order of keys you have just been practising.

Further Starting Points

(i)

Ex. 91

[repeat bars 1 and 2]

(ii)

Ex. 92 March 1

Continue for another eight bars, relating them rhythmically to the first eight but starting the melody on a different degree of the tonic chord.

(iii)

Ex. 93 March 2

(iv)

Ex. 94 **Lullaby**

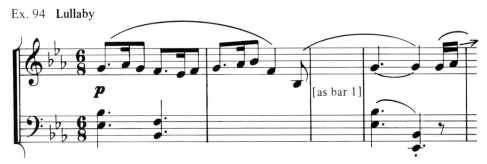

Monotonous bass registration at the outset will suggest the rocking movement. Later you can vary it.

Ornamentation

(i)   As a framework for these exercises use the first five notes of any scale, ascending and descending. Come to rest on the 2nd degree:

Ex. 95

Play either a tonic or dominant 5th under *every* note, arranging the registration so that the bass is shapely and purposeful. Repeat the two bars in the dominant key.

(ii)   Improvisation reveals why musical short-cut signs have been developed as labour-saving devices where a single idea involves a number of notes. You have already become familiar with the mordents (p. 31) played as triplets. The first mordents written down in the 17th century had short-cut signs, ∿ for upper mordent and ∿ for lower mordent: these were not played as triplets, however, but as ♩♬ and ♩♬. But the three notes form one idea, which can be played slowly or quickly, and the term 'mordent' will be used here to describe any alternation of a note with its neighbour in any rhythmic pattern, such as ♪♪♪, ♪♪♩, ♪♪♩, ♩.♪♪ . Decorate Ex. 95 with lower mordents in the ascending bar and upper mordents in the descending bar, over the same bass 5ths:

Ex. 96

(iii)   A mordent may use either the next-door note in the scale (called a 'tonal' ornament) or a next-door note *outside* the scale a semitone away (called 'chromatic'):

Ex. 97

Play this again, choosing tonal or chromatic mordents and mixing them as you please. Repeat this time in the key of the 4th degree (F).

(iv)   A combination of upper and lower ornaments is known as a *turn* with the sign ∾ meaning ♪. Spaced evenly, the turn may be used as a basis for improvising a piece in $\frac{5}{8}$ beginning:

Ex. 98

Use tonal or chromatic inflections.

(v)   Experiment with ornamented broken chords of I and V, starting with a low left-hand 5th and covering a wide range of registration of 5ths on the indicated changes of chord:

Ex. 99

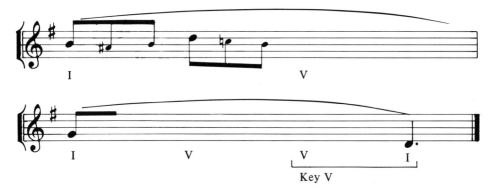

Bar 1   ascend the tonic arpeggio, decorating with lower mordents.

Bar 2   descend the dominant arpeggio, decorating with either mordent.

Bar 3   repeat the given half-bar melodic phrase sequentially, one degree lower.

Bar 4   descend the scale with upper mordents, ending in the dominant key.

Then repeat the whole in the dominant key and continue as you wish. You may also decorate the same exercise with turns, beginning:

Ex. 100

Repertory Examples

(i)   Look again at Ex. 80 (p. 37). Although Rameau keeps the tonic 5th constant, many bars suggest a dominant 5th as well. Play the example again and listen for dominant harmony. Then notice the number of mordents written out as ♪♫♩ in the melody. These are all simple decorations of the kind you have practised in this chapter.

(ii)

Ex. 101   Impromptu, op. 90 no. 2: opening   *F. Schubert*

Notice the triplet mordent in bars 3 and 4, each carrying a chromatic passing note.

(iii)

Ex. 102 **Bagatelle, op. 33 no. 3: bars as numbered**   *L. van Beethoven*

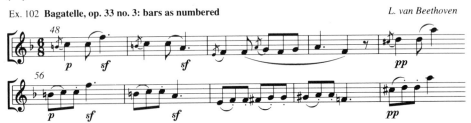

First Beethoven puts the appoggiatura before the beat, with a diagonal line through the tail to show it: this is then called an 'acciaccatura' (= crushed together). Later he reverts to the longer appoggiatura and writes it out in full, phrased to emphasise its discord and release. (The bass is shown in Ex. 83.)

(iv)

Ex. 103 **Die Kunst der Fingerfertigkeit, op. 740 no. 42: opening**   *C. Czerny*

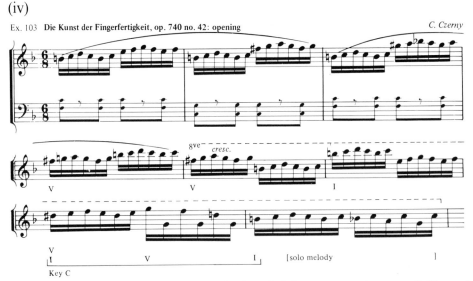

This melodic pattern consists entirely of rising appoggiaturas followed by a turn in each unit. The left hand can play tonic and dominant 5ths to outline the underlying harmony. At the end, Czerny uses another well-known device to return to the tonic key (see p. 3).

Further Ornamentation

(i)   Play the first five notes of the scale of C with a change of 5th under every note, as in Ex. 95. Then decorate each degree with an upper mordent, as a triplet. Now omit the first note and place the middle note *on* the beat, so it becomes an appoggiatura. This makes a discord with the bass, causing a tension which is released when that note falls, to be 'resolved' on to the note belonging to the chord. Play appoggiaturas above each degree of the original scale; musical phrasing and gradation of tone are essential to making sense of this:

Ex. 104

(ii) Repeat the same passage with appoggiaturas *below* each harmony note. As with mordents, chromatic may sometimes be preferred to tonal appoggiaturas. Such chromatic notes, or 'accidentals', do not alter the key of the piece, but you may occasionally wish to alter the bass registration.

(iii) The short-cut way to indicate such appoggiaturas was to print them in small notes, showing that they were *ornaments* in front of harmony notes, delaying the harmony note itself, as in:

Ex. 105   Piano Sonata, K330: slow movement, bars 11 - 12   *W. A. Mozart*

Play this as it is meant to sound, *i.e.* with the third-beat melody notes in four equal ♪ s. The long appoggiatura in the second bar is written out (see *SaK*, p. 244).

(iv) In simple time you will need to think more quickly. Play upper or lower appoggiaturas on each beat in the first two bars, then add the 5ths below that belong to the *harmony* of each printed note in the melody:

Ex. 106

[What happens here?]

49

(v)   Taking this piece as a pattern, improvise one of your own using all the ornaments practised in this chapter:

Ex. 107

Filling out the Texture

Here are some starting points based on the processes in *SaK*, pp. 125–127.

(i)   To prepare for this texture, practise broken chords in 10ths like this:

Ex. 108

Such chords can be used like a harp accompaniment, rippled up lightly with an unstrained, relaxed hand and a little support from the pedal:

Ex. 109

Apply this texture also to Ex. 86.

(ii)

Ex. 110 **Skipping**

Ex. 111 **Running**

Ex. 112 **Rocking**

Ex. 113 **Carol**

Sometimes you will need to change the harmony within the bar in this piece. Extend it with a section using chords I and V in the dominant key.

(iii) *SaK*, p. 126, explains the 'two-note' pattern which expresses dominant seventh and tonic harmonies in a simple, flowing texture. The closeness of the left-hand notes makes this a particularly suitable texture for small hands. Improvise a melody over landscaping 5ths, to establish the harmonies, then see if you can repeat it, substituting the two-note accompaniment for the 5ths. Here is a starting point which shows both landscaping 5ths and accompaniment:

Ex. 114

The *d″* in the melody with *c* in the accompaniment will not sound harsh if the accompaniment is musically played, with the lilting pattern emphasising each ♩ and the dominant pivot ♪s light and soft.

Ex. 115

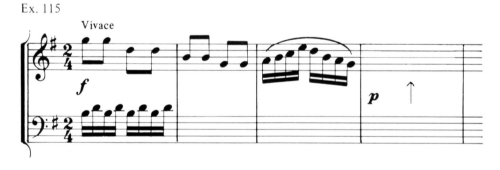

Ex. 116

molto cantabile

(iv) Improvise your own pieces on this pattern, in various keys.

These processes enable you to make an extended piece, *most* of which will be successful: it is then not difficult to modify any little areas which would be improved by small changes. To retain self-confidence and stylistic consistency are the important things.

Folio

Your work on this chapter should provide a nice variety of short pieces for your folio, perhaps including some melodies as settings of nursery rhymes or folk song words.

5 THREE-CHORD IMPROVISATION

(*SaK 4*)

Players dissatisfied with their improvisation who attribute this to using 'just I, IV and V' are under a misapprehension. In most music of the 18th and 19th centuries these 'primary' chords predominate, which is what harmonic landscaping defines (see *SaK*, pp. 64–65). The real reason why improvisation restricted to these three chords may indeed be poor lies not in those chords themselves but in *how they are used*. Your dissatisfaction is more likely to be due to:

(a) failure to give priority of thought to making a melody,
(b) preoccupation with harmony in terms of chords,
(c) chords following each other in too quick succession, with no melody flowing between,
(d) chords arranged in an unvaried texture of hymn-like solidity.

There are five ways to provide contrast and variety in improvisation:

> Change dynamics
> Change register
> Change key
> Change harmony
> Change texture

You have already used all of these, with as yet only two changes of harmony, chords I and V. Those two chords were first introduced in *SaK*, pp. 37–38, each applied to half of the two-verse structure of 'Girls and Boys Come Out to Play'. It is also best to start using the subdominant, chord IV, in a structural capacity, to provide a contrast in the third quarter of a piece in which the first half uses only chords I and V. This is how it occurs in many folk songs (see 'Ho-La-Hi', *SaK*, p. 58). So you can use chord IV to extend pieces you improvised in the last chapter. Melodically, many tunes run around the first five degrees of the scale for the first half; then the need for a lift in the third quarter generates a rise to the 6th degree and above, and it is here that chord IV is usually appropriate. Experience this by adding bass 5ths to these two melodies:

(i)

Ex. 117

[repeat bar 1]

[imitate bar 1]

(ii)

Ex. 118

[repeat phrase 1]

[imitate phrase 1]   [sequence]

The 6th degree calls for chord IV more often than the 4th degree itself does. For the 4th degree in a melody is equally part of the dominant seventh (V^7) as of chord IV, and V^7 may often be the harmony you wish to hear at that point. In the penultimate bar of (i) above, try using a single bass 5th throughout. Only if you use two 5ths in that bar is subdominant bass appropriate, to precede V (quickening the harmonic pace like this is usually reserved for main cadences) but chord IV is vital to the structure of the piece in phrase three.

These short pieces are constructed on a common formula which you can now use in your improvisation: exposition (involving some repetition); development section (using the original idea); and a recapitulation (complete or shortened). Using this structure you will soon learn to give chord IV its appropriate place. Play Ex. 86 (p. 42) again (using only V and I) and begin an added section like this:

Ex. 119

[one chord]

Then extend several other pieces in chapter 4 by the same process.

Starting Points

Use these starting points to include chord IV as initiator of a third section of a piece, or as a brief forerunner to V or HXB at a main cadence. Concentrate on melody and keep the 5ths sparse; sometimes you may need two in a bar, but not more. Extend pieces or sections by repetition in related keys.

(i)   Play left-hand HXB preceded by a 4th degree solo note under every phrase of this piece. Vary the register of the bass:

Ex. 120

Finish with a couple more phrases. Notice how you can avoid a sense of finality by ending a phrase on the 3rd degree of the scale instead of the keynote (bar 2), and that you can use the 4th degree bass under the 2nd degree (end of bar 3).

(ii)   Choose another key and improvise a melody with phrases starting on various degrees of the scale involved in the chord of IV, proceeding upwards or downwards. Note also the possibility of appoggiaturas (as at the beginning of the last phrase above, *b″—a″* over bass *f*). Use 5ths and single-note bass.

Continue the following starting points, using sparse bass 5ths and the occasional single-note cadential bass when you feel it is really needed.

(iii)

Ex. 121

Poco marcato

[new 5th]

Keep to continuous ♩s in the melody, well structured in phrase lengths and allowing the occasional longer note at a phrase ending. Play at a walking pace.

(iv)

Ex. 122   **March**

(v)

Ex. 123   **Lullaby**

(vi)

Ex. 124

sempre staccato

Keep to continuous ♪s in the melody at a running pace, over 5ths which change when the melody needs them to.

(vii)

Ex. 125 **Mazurka**

Try both possible 5ths at the beginning and choose the one you prefer. Finish with a cadence in the typical mazurka rhythm ending on a second beat like this:

Ex. 126

Do you think the chord in the penultimate bar should be IV or V? Try both. There should, of course, be only one 5th under the final bar, as the *e'* is an appoggiatura.

Texturing Chords I, V and IV

(i)

Ex. 127 **Skipping**

When you have fixed your melody and harmony by 5ths, texture the piece by the extended broken-chord treatment, as in Ex. 110 (p. 51).

Improvise with this texture straight away if you can. After the first eight bars, repeat them in the dominant key. Continue, making use of chord IV in the new key. Then find your way back to the tonic key. Chord IV of the tonic key, used melodically, will help you to do this, as a natural D will cancel the sharp D which has been the leading note of the dominant key.

(ii)

Ex. 128 **Dotted Skip**

Be careful to maintain the dotted rhythm without slipping into triplets.

(a) Accompany with 5ths.
(b) Convert the 5ths to extended broken chords in continuous ♪ s. This will aid accurate playing of the dotted rhythm.
(c) Texture the same harmonies as a two-note accompaniment (illustrated in Ex. 115, p. 52) using 4th to 6th degrees to maintain the same style for chord IV.

(iii)

Ex. 129

Vivace

[bass as bar 2]

Notice that the 6th degree in the melody occurs first as part of chord IV, then accompanied by V^7.

(iv)

Ex. 130

Lullaby

59

(v)

Ex. 131

Use 5ths and HXB. Then try making a version in two-part counterpoint on the lines of chapter 2. The bass should, for the most part, move slower than the treble.

(vi)

Ex. 132

[sequence]

The 5ths should move at a slow pace for the first two bars. Then raise the melody an octave and texture the harmonies in extended broken chords in ♪♪♪♪ until the pace of change only allows for each 5th to be broken into ♪♪ .

(vii)

Ex. 133

Later in the piece, adapt bar 1 to rise melodically instead of falling and see where that leads you.

(viii)

Ex. 134

[sequence

one third lower]   [repeat phrase 1]

Use the harp-style accompaniment. Do not include more than three 'spread' notes in the left-hand chords. Listen carefully to the pedalling to avoid a smudgy overlap between chords. When the rhythmic structure requires two chords but only one harmony, play the chord twice in the bar. The sequential passage should use only one chord per bar. Bar 7 reveals that chord I of any key is chord IV of its dominant key. Invent more pieces in this style.

(ix)

Ex. 135

Ex. 136

Ex. 137

All these five-note patterns may be inverted, and you can use a broken chord accompaniment. To add the 6th degree as passing note and as an appoggiatura makes a pleasing final cadence:

Ex. 138

(x)

Ex. 139

Use the broken chord accompaniment as in Ex. 133, in the rhythm

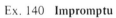. After eight bars, continue with subdominant harmony.

(xi)

Ex. 140 **Impromptu**

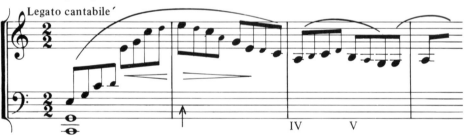

Although two chords are suggested in bar 3, do not use many two-chord bars, or the piece will lose its underlying phrase structure. The basic pattern can be inverted:

Ex. 141

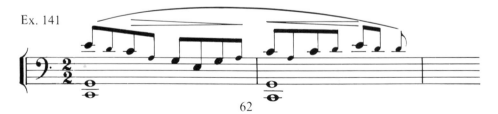

In these two starting points the melody is based on a broken chord: to clarify this the notes outside the chord (unaccented passing notes) are printed small. As you continue, put some on the beat, as 'accented passing notes', another name for appoggiaturas.

Further Ornamentation

(i)   On page 45 you harmonised the first five degrees of the major scale with a bass 5th *under every degree*, using chords I and V only. Now treat the full ascending major scale in the same way, including chord IV as a bass 5th where it seems applicable:

Ex. 142

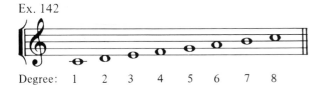

Degree: 1   2   3   4   5   6   7   8

Avoid chords IV and V running parallel with the direction of the melody (see *Sa K*, p. 61). Memorise this passage.
(ii)   Play the scale over the harmonising 5ths, but precede each melodic degree with an upper appoggiatura, decorating the degree, like this:

Ex. 143

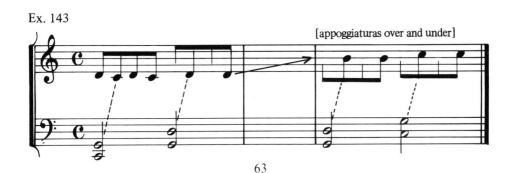

[appoggiaturas over and under]

(iii)

Ex. 144

Include appoggiaturas in your improvisation; these can be over or under any of the notes belonging to each of the three chords. This reveals again how vital it is not to include the 3rds of chords in the bass, as you will hear if you do add them (see *SaK*, p. 40, Ex. 11b).

Folio

Add some results of your improvisations on this chapter. Remember that you can make a piece in ternary form by following one short piece with another contrasting one and then repeating the first, in full or shortened.

6 FOUR-CHORD IMPROVISATION

(*SaK 5,11*)

The basic scale of many modal melodies consists of the first five degrees of the minor scale, plus the 7th degree a tone below the tonic:

Ex. 145

Degree: 1 2 3 4 5 4 3 2 1   7

Play this interval pattern from *d'*, *a'*, *e'*, *g'* and *c'*. The roots of the four main chords for landscaping are on degrees 1, 3, 5 and 7. These four chords, being a mixture of major and minor, offer a particularly rich harmonic vocabulary and provide a wider choice than the diatonic primaries. But the wider the choice, the more you need to listen carefully so that what you play matches the sound which, consciously or not, you pre-hear associated with your melody.

The simplest modal melodies can often be harmonised on chords I and VII only. Accompany this example by bass 5ths of I and VII, then transpose it to the modes on *a'*, then on *e'*, *g'* and *c'*:

Ex. 146

I   VII

Play the passage at the same five pitches, decorating each beat with upper or lower mordents, in this rhythm:

Ex. 147

If you found it natural to raise the 7th degree in the first mordent you would be putting into practice one of the *musica ficta* variants traditionally associated with modal music (*SaK*, pp. 79–81).

Returning to example 146, substitute the bass 5th of chord V for chord VII. Then arrange the phrase with a mixture of the *three* bass 5ths and play it at all five pitches. Finally, substitute the bass 5th of chord III for chord I at the only possible place. This might alter your choice of the next chord. Play the phrase using all *four* bass 5ths at all five pitches.

Starting Points

In continuing these melodic openings there is no reason why you cannot include the 6th degree which, like the 7th, is variable on the *musica ficta* principle. The four landscaping 5ths can be mixed up as you please as the juxtaposition of major and minor chords is typical of modal harmony. While you are enjoying your own modal improvisations you will be learning at first hand how this kind of mixture inevitably destroys major harmonisation, converting it to modal. This is why it is *so* important to start work in any tonality using only the principal chords before you include any subsidiary chords which may distort it.

(i)

Ex. 148

After eight bars, start a second section like this:

Ex. 149

Then treat this phrase sequentially from *d'*: continue as you wish.

(ii)

Ex. 150

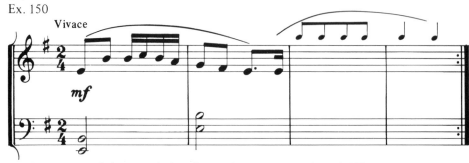

Make sequential use of the first phrase over chord III at some stage.

66

(iii)

Ex. 151 **Swinging**

Use tonic 5th only for a long stretch, changing the 5th for another long stretch, then return to the first stretch. Make a piece in ternary form by adding a contrasting section in C major (chord III) then repeat the first section. Guard against slipping into $\frac{6}{8}$.

(iv)

Ex. 152

(v)

Ex. 153

Energico

This is another opening for the 'long-stretch' treatment. Use it to improvise another piece in the same form as Ex. 151. Change the register for at least one stretch and add a coda experimenting with the 6th degree of the scale like this:

Ex. 154

Choose whether to end with no 3rd in the final chord (as commonly found in modal music) or whether to add a *g* in the right hand, or raise it to *g♯*—the *Tierce de Picardie* of the modal period (see *SaK*, p. 80).

(vi)

Ex. 155

Establish a clear structure in the melody by using long notes at the end of most phrases.

(vii)

Ex. 156

Retain tonic harmony for the whole first phrase. The second phrase, though imitative, might change its chord at the end of the phrase.

(viii)
Ex. 157

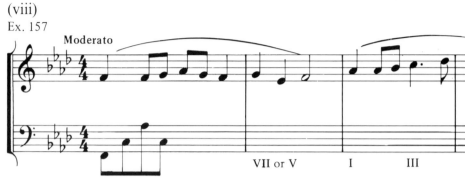

(ix)
In the three following improvisations the variable 6th degree may lead you to want chord IV as an extra subsidiary harmony:

(a)
Ex. 158

(b)
Ex. 159

(c)
Ex. 160

(x)

Ex. 161

Ripple the bass chords easily in harp style. In the three short phrases which drop to *e'*, vary the accompanying chords. As you continue, move into the E mode, in which you could imitate the short phrases.

(xi)

Ex. 162

Use this melodic pattern on each of the principal modal chords in turn, melody and bass ascending crescendo and descending diminuendo. Play in two, three, four or five beats to the bar. Notice how well the passing note at the end of the pattern of four ♪s links to the next chord, both on ascent and descent. Then enrich the accompaniment, spreading each chord like this:

Ex. 163

This left-hand arpeggio is constructed strictly on the order of the harmonic series, with triad over 5th, producing the most resonant sound.

Contrapuntal and Other Textures

(i)

Ex. 164

This passage enables you to use modal harmonies in a contrapuntal texture. The three-note motif of chapter 2 may now be seen in harmonic terms as running over the scalic notes of one of the thirds in a triad, usually the lower third. The framework is an extended scale, which should first be treated by 'dehydration'. Normally, in landscaping, you use 5ths sparsely because the melody is regarded as several notes flowing within each harmony. 'Dehydration' is a reverse preparatory process in which *every* note is given a 5th, because the passage will then be brought to life by expansion into a flowing texture (in this case in the bass) within the area of each 5th, as a counterpoint to the melody's long notes.

(a) First set each ♩ of the scalic notes with a modal bass 5th.
(b) Transform the bass into a four-note pattern in each beat, using the lower third of the relevant chord, as in the bottom

stave of the example. Good registration of the 5ths will benefit the counterpoint. You may want to try improvising a contrapuntal bass like this straight away; but if you are not happy with it, always go back to landscaping. Improvise a firm bass ending, not necessarily on this pattern.

(ii)

Ex. 165

Treat this descending scale in the same way as example 164. If you can play the right-hand part as three-note chords (*SaK*, pp. 193–196) add their weight to the texture. Make sure first that your harmonies are fully defined in the two-part texture.

(iii)

Ex. 166

This is the scale of the E flat mode, with the 6th degree not raised. Play it several times, then improvise a two-part piece, $\frac{3}{4}$ over $\frac{6}{8}$, which you will find quite easy:

Ex. 167

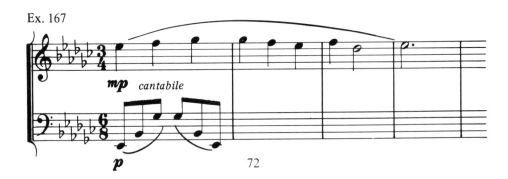

(iv)

Ex. 168 **Pavane**

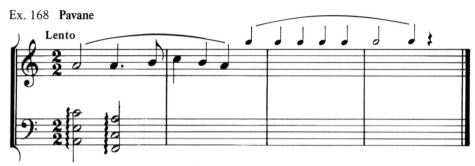

Use 5ths alone in the fourth bar, the two beats being identical and simply a matter of rhythmic repetition. Then try filling out the chords like this (*SaK*, p. 143):

Ex. 169

Folio

Add some modal pieces. These might be for country dances (for examples, see *SaK*, pp. 73 and 148–9) or early court dances (*SaK*, p. 83). You might find an Elizabethan poem and give it a modal melody with accompaniment.

7 SIX-CHORD IMPROVISATION

(*SaK* 6,12,13)

The four main chords with which you improvised in the previous chapter
were mixed more or less haphazardly to give the music its modal
character. But often you will have found yourself pairing the two minor
chords together and the two major chords together, especially in
accompanying sequential melody. Those pairings could briefly indicate
chords I and V of a minor key and chords I and V of its relative major. In
diatonic minor music chord IV, the subdominant, of the minor key and
that of its relative major are added, making six chords in all:

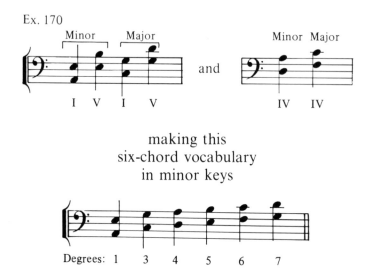

The only missing chord is that on the 2nd degree of the minor scale,
which is also the 7th degree of the relative major. The 5th above this
degree (*b'* in A minor/C major) is a diminished interval whose
generating 5th in the harmonic series is lower down, and only perfect
5ths are relevant to harmonic landscaping. These six chords need to be
segregated as the three minor and three major primary chords in any
mainly minor piece (see *SaK*, pp. 92–93). Improvising is easier than
harmonising a given minor melody, because *you* choose where to play
major areas.

Starting Points

(i)   Remember that in minor *melodies* degrees 6 and 7 are variable, though bass 5ths built on those degrees are not (see the last two 5ths in Ex. 170). Degrees 6 and 7 (being the 3rds of those two chords) will be open to your choice in the melody, as in this example:

Ex. 171

[Relative major]

Continue with a section in the relative major, using the 5ths of the three major primary chords.

(ii)

Ex. 172 **Minuet**

Set this first phrase with one bass 5th per bar. Continue by imitating it in its relative major key with the appropriate 5ths. Then play this phrase with 5ths:

Ex. 173 **[Minuet]**

and imitate it in the original minor key, choosing which inflection of degrees 6 and 7 you prefer. Repeat the original phrase, perhaps modifying the last two bars. You can then extend the piece further with a new section in the relative major and recapitulate the opening in the minor, ending as you wish.

(iii)

Ex. 174 **Gavotte**

To establish and maintain the characteristic rhythm of the gavotte the anacrusic half-bars which begin each two-bar phrase should be unaccompanied, at least for a while. Later the harmonic pace may quicken, with half-bar changes of 5th—but be careful not to lose the basic anacrusic structure. Include a section in the relative major and a recapitulation in the minor.

(iv)

Ex. 175 **March**

Complete a four-bar phrase. Base the next four bars on imitation of the initial bars in the relative major. Now make an approximate inversion of the original two-bar theme, still in the major, by *descending* from the top of the chord in the rhythm of bar 1. Let the final four bars reproduce this inversion in the original key, before you add a final cadence. You may strengthen the march by adding the 3rd of each chord, spread harp-style, beneath the melody now raised an octave. You will need quite a lot of pedal support to sustain the spread chords and add resonance.

(v)

Ex. 176

Bar 5 indicates appoggiaturas, so the *second* in each pair is the harmony note which indicates the relevant 5th. Use this opening as a chance to include more ornamentation, perhaps with a turn around the $b\natural'$ in the first bar and a few mordents in the manner of Rameau (page 37).

Contrapuntal Improvisation

You have seen how harmony and counterpoint are often interlinked. *Sa K*, pp. 154–157 introduced the conversion of harmonic landscaping to counterpoint. These starting points will help you to combine the two approaches in improvisation.

(i)

Ex. 177

[repeat bars 1 and 2]   *dim.*

   (a)   Play this melody, then landscape the harmonies with 5ths.
   (b)   Without thinking of the landscaping, treat all suitable bars by inverted 3-note counterpoint, beginning:

Ex. 178

When the melody changes to equal ♩s let the left hand play the dotted rhythm. Keep the bass moving under long melody notes to link the phrases.

77

(c)   Landscape with 5ths again, to match the harmonies suggested by your counterpoint. If these 5ths differ from those you first played, compare the difference and make a choice.

(d)   Continue the piece freely, using any contrapuntal devices you like. You might start:

Ex. 179

Work towards a modulation to the dominant key, ending with a return to E flat. Then recapitulate the first section of the original C minor melody above.

(e)   See if you can now play the whole piece from memory.

(ii)

Ex. 180

Linking the three-note motif with HXB via the 4th degree like this is extremely useful as a contrapuntal bass line, adaptable to any other rhythm.

(a)   Start a piece in this way and repeat your first section in the relative major.

(b)   Continue with a section on the same bass pattern in the dominant minor key, treated sequentially in *its* relative major, beginning:

Ex. 181

(iii)

Ex. 182

The 3-note motif here represents *one* chord. But it can also substitute as a bass for *two* chords:

Ex. 183

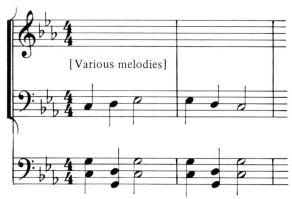

[Various melodies]

Landscaping can be turned into a single-line bass in this way, either for a chordal texture (*SaK*, p. 204) or a contrapuntal texture (*SaK*, p. 155). Such a single-line bass can lighten the texture when the harmonic pace changes quickly and successive 5ths (root positions) seem heavy. Re-play example 176 fast, substituting a 3-note single-line bass like this for the previous I-V-I 5ths. Then vary ensuing note lengths in the bass melody. A 3-note motif on any consecutive degrees of the major or minor scale can replace two chords in this way (*SaK*, p. 204). Working contrapuntally you will begin to feel how your bass can move without your needing to think chordally.

(iv)

Ex. 184 **Alla Mazurka**

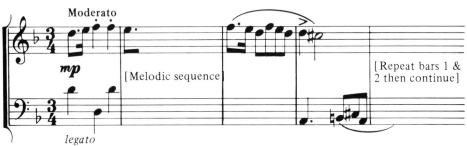

Treat this melody with an octave bass, alternating the notes in either direction. Use the notes which would be at the bottom of the relevant 5ths if you were landscaping; or try a descending scalic octave bass. (Small hands can substitute repeated single notes.) Link the phrases as in bar 4. These links can be varied with a further passing note, ascending or descending towards the starting note of the next phrase, which may be in the same or a related key:

Ex. 185a   Ex. 185b

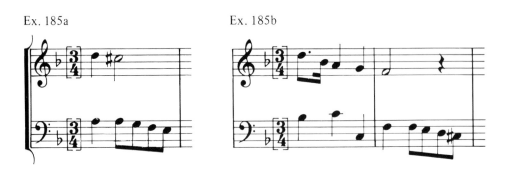

(a) could lead to either key. Try both. (b) will lead you back from relative major to minor.

(v)

Ex. 186 **Minuet from** *Notebook for Anna Magdalena* **(BWVa 132)**   *J. S. Bach*

Improvise a contrapuntal bass to this melody, keeping it moving where the melody is static. Prior landscaping with sparse 5ths may help you to do this. When you have completed your contrapuntal version, compare it with a copy of Bach's original.

Further Starting Points

(i)

Ex. 187

Use the two-note accompaniment pattern. Complete a four-bar phrase, then imitate it in the relative major. For the next section cross hands, playing the melody at the same pitch or an octave lower with the right hand and the accompanying pattern two octaves higher with the left hand. In a further section, remember how chord IV can make a welcome change from I and V, so start on subdominant harmony in the major and imitate it in the minor. As the initial theme covers a small range of notes, later sections could use a wider melodic span.

(ii)
Ex. 188

Improvise a simple study on this theme to gain confidence in playing the cross-rhythm (see page 16).

Ex. 189 **Nocturne**

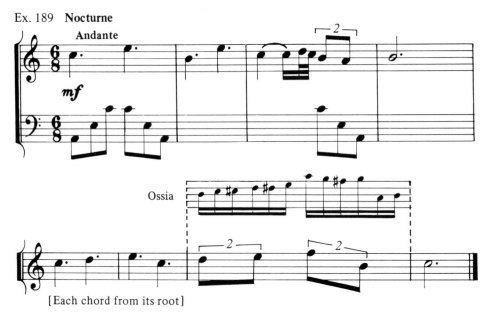

[Each chord from its root]

The cross-rhythm of your study may now be incorporated into a piece as shown in this example. The *Ossia* decoration of the melody in bar 7 is easy to play as there is no cross-rhythm with the left hand. Notation often makes things look harder than they are. In developing your improvising skill you will find that such things as wide leaps, which you may find nerve-racking from notation, become simple because *you* are inventing them and know where you are going. Increased physical familiarity with the keyboard helps confidence in sight reading too.

In your Nocturne, change keys freely, so long as it makes sense to you and you eventually return to the tonic key. Notice how easily a raised 3rd (*c#'*) in the tonic chord of A minor provides chord V in D minor, the subdominant key:

82

Ex. 190

Two more familiar harmonic devices may be incorporated in this
piece at the end: the interrupted cadence, V–VI, in both minor and
major keys (*SaK*, p. 118, Ex. 52) and the addition of a major 3rd in the
final chord of a minor piece, the *Tierce de Picardie*, here extended to the
whole final *section*—a chord expanded into a key:

Ex. 191

(iii)

Ex. 192

Improvise a piece in ternary form. Vary the spacing of the registration. Use relative major, also a later section in the *tonic* major, beginning:

Ex. 193

Incorporate a long-note trill somewhere, in either hand (starting on the upper note). Contrary-motion scale passages can also be included, one hand moving in while the other uses .

(iv)

Ex. 194

Improvise an accompaniment with *both* hands (*SaK*, pp. 144–5) for an instrumental or song melody of your own, or use this beginning. The right hand of the accompaniment need not always play the same degrees, 5th and 3rd, of each chord; to keep the right-hand position in bar 3 closer to that in bar 2 will be more satisfactory:

Ex. 195

Even without an *e* in bar 3 there is no doubt that the chord is A minor.

Folio

(i)   Write out a contrapuntal piece in simple binary form, first improvised at the keyboard. The first section should modulate from minor to relative major (with repeat sign) and the second section should start with some development before returning to the original minor in a recapitulation (also with repeat sign).

(ii)   Add any other successful improvisations to your collection. If you need more starting points remember that most of the major ones in chapters 4 and 5 can be adapted for use in the tonic minor. See how many of the devices shown in these first seven chapters you have employed.

8 TOPPING UP

(*SaK 7, 8*)

Starting Points

Most of these starting points may be developed as complete short pieces in ternary or rondo form: a few are more suited to passage-work areas, such as 'bridge passages' and codas: all will need practice to master the manual facility to improvise on each texture.

(i)

Ex. 196

L.H. *legato*

Continue to improvise in thirds, divided between the hands. Then drop the left-hand part an octave and exchange rhythms so that it plays the ♪♪♪ a tenth below the right hand.

(ii)

Ex. 197

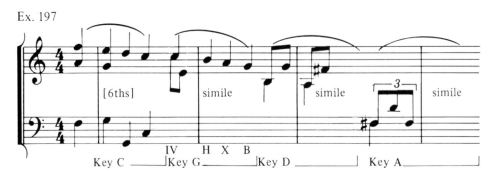

Enjoy the feeling of playing continuous 6ths over a four-note cadence (4 + HXB) on these various rhythmic patterns, through a series of keys (*SaK*, pp. 107–109). Then improvise on a similar bass, beginning:

Ex. 198

[3rds]   [3rds]

Key G _____

The final unison *g'* might then be used as the 4th degree of D major, but try playing the next pair of keys as D minor and A minor.

(iii)

Ex. 199

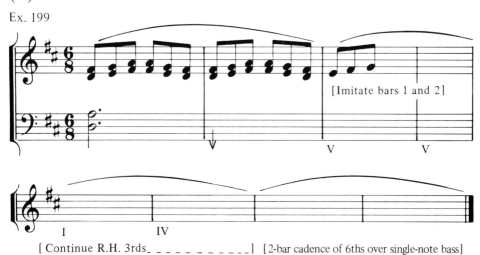

[Imitate bars 1 and 2]

V   V

I   IV

[Continue R.H. 3rds _ _ _ _ _ _ _ _ _ _] [2-bar cadence of 6ths over single-note bass]

The clue to extending such a passage is *not* to sit down at the end, wondering what to do next:

Ex. 200

[6ths over single-note bass]

but to keep the texture moving with a link like this:

Ex. 201

[6ths]

H   X   B

This leads well into a repeat of your initial eight bars in another key—
dominant or relative minor: or subdominant if you ease the transition
by using the present tonic chord as dominant 7th of the new key:

Ex. 202

[6ths]

You might develop the piece like this:

  (a) Repeat bars 1–6 in the relative minor. Use the original cadence
       in bars 7–8 to come back to D major, but raise the register of
       the second-beat 6ths. This will provide a highlight to the whole
       piece and bring you back to the original link bar in a higher
       register.
  (b) Repeat bars 1–7 in the dominant with HXB cadence. Let bar 8
       of this section link back (down or up) to the tonic key.
  (c) Repeat the original eight bars with a 'cross-hand' variation:
       instead of dropping in register, let the repeated bass 5th cross
       above the right hand, first in alternate bars, then on second
       beats.
  (d) As a coda, play flowing 6ths divided between the two hands
       inside sustained outer keynotes:

Ex. 203

This is called a tonic pedal bass (see *SaK*, p. 36).
    A long piece of this kind has plenty of scope for varying the dynamics
in the different sections.

88

(iv)

Ex. 204 **March**

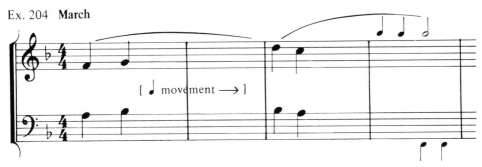

[♩ movement →]

(v)

Ex. 205 **Running**

p

[3rds]

(vi)

Ex. 206 **Skipping**

R.H.

L.H.

Make each ♩ staccato, leaping off the keys as you would skip off the ground. Continue the sequence down the scale, ending with a cadence like this:

Ex. 207

89

Adapting Ex. 206:
- (a) Experiment with an ascending pattern: four steps up, drop two degrees, then climb again.
- (b) Experiment with the descending pattern, converting it to a three-beat unit ($\frac{9}{8}$ time), then treat it sequentially in either direction.
- (c) Convert (b) to combine skipping and walking rhythms by dropping the left hand one or two octaves to play legato ♩·s. Use the keys of D or C.
- (d) Exchange the rhythmic elements like this:

Ex. 208

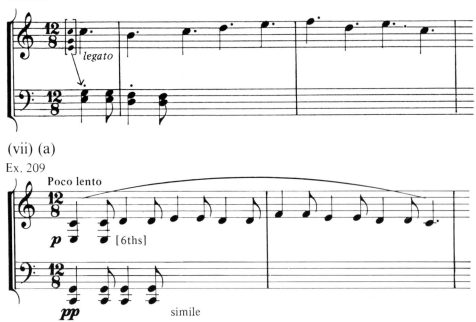

(vii) (a)

Ex. 209

Repeat in the subdominant. Later, try 3rds over a tonic pedal in various keys.

(b)

Ex. 210

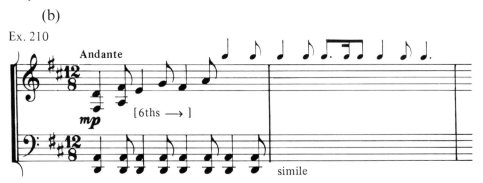

Repeat in the dominant and develop from there.

(c)

Ex. 211

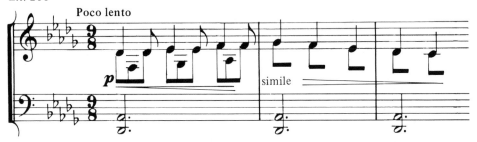

Repeat a four-bar phrase in the subdominant before continuing.

(d)

Ex. 212

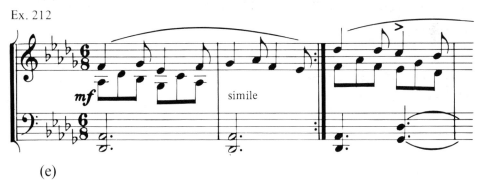

(e)

Ex. 213

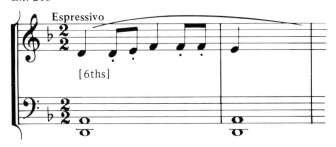

Repeat in the relative major key after four bars, then continue.

(viii)(a)

Ex. 214

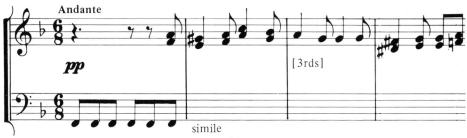

(b)

Ex. 215

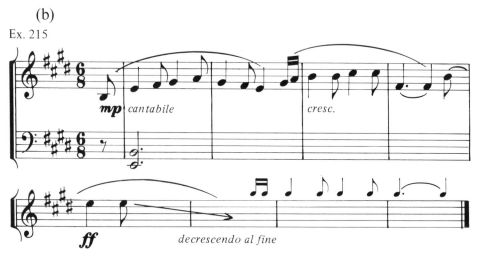

Use a mixture of right-hand 6ths and 3rds. Substitute an octave bass for a bass 5th in the left hand occasionally. Repeat your eight-bar phrase in the tonic minor, ending with a *Tierce de Picardie*.

(ix)

Ex. 216

Ex. 217

Ex. 218

From each opening, repeat a four-bar phrase in the dominant—major or minor? (*SaK*, p. 91, last paragraph.)

(x) (a)

Ex. 219 **Siciliano**

(b)

Ex. 220 **Gallop**

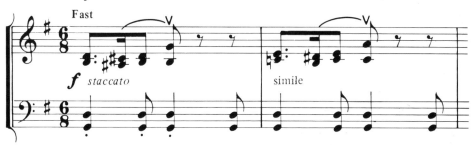

(xi)

Ex. 221 **Allegro brillante**

(a) Reverse the rhythmic pattern of the two hands, dropping the lower part an octave, like this:

Ex. 222

L.H.

(b) Return to Ex. 221 and introduce some chromatic notes. These may be temporary and soon cancelled again, making only a fleeting reference to another key, like a train passing a village without stopping:

Ex. 223

(c) Change to triple time and make chromatic alterations at the points marked ★ :

Ex. 224

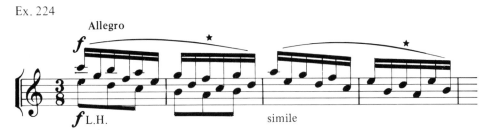

(d) After these four bars add a two-bar cadence re-establishing C major. Repeat the four bars, adding two bars to establish E minor. Then prolong the passage to modulate to G major. Repeat, establishing modulations to, respectively, A minor, F major and D minor, by chromatic changes in either hand.

Further Starting Points

(i)

Ex. 225 **Tango**

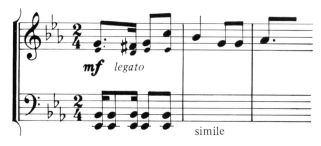

Only change the 5th when you feel it essential. Sometimes use 3rds, sometimes 6ths, in the right hand.

94

(ii)

Ex. 226 **Bavarian Landler**

(iii)

Ex. 227

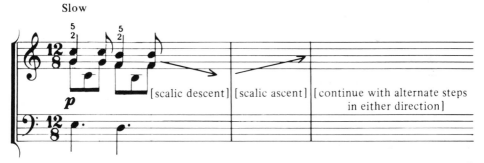

(iv) Improvise a piece of 'programme music' for a mime of Sisyphus, whose punishment in the underworld was to push a marble block uphill which, as soon as it reached the top, always rolled down again:

Ex. 228

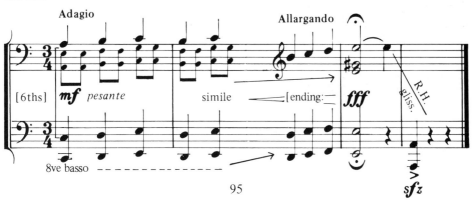

(v)

Ex. 229

Try a second improvisation on this opening, starting with the chord of C *minor* and proceed as your ear dictates. Then try chromatic modifications of bars 2 or 3 and follow where they lead.

(vi)

Ex. 230

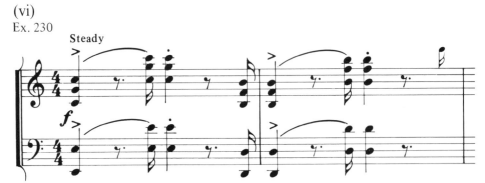

Continue the progression down the scale. To avoid becoming confused by the wide leaps, cling slightly to the *lowest* note of the upper pair of chords in each hand, feeling and visualising that the *highest* note of your next chord will be the one below the note you are clinging to, *i.e.* right-hand little finger will play the note below the right-hand thumb-note as you drop the octave, and vice versa for the left hand.

(vii)

Ex. 231

This is a series of $^6_3$ chords (a 6th with a 3rd between). Experiment with different registers and include descending sequences.

(viii)(a)

Ex. 232

Play this alternation of 3rds and 6ths as written. Then raise the lower notes marked ★ chromatically, and see what you can do with this sequential framework.

(b)

Ex. 233

This is another way of alternating 3rds and 6ths for a contrapuntal improvisation. Experiment with melodic inversion of either interval and possible rhythmic inversions.

(ix) Improvise a piece on $^6_3$ chords over a tonic pedal, starting like this:

Ex. 234

After a while, move to a dominant pedal and back again.

Ornamentation with 3rds and 6ths

Play an ascending scale of appoggiaturas over bass 5ths beginning:

Ex. 235

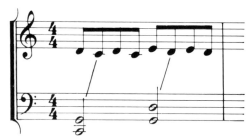

(i)   Omit the bass 5th and double every melody note with a 6th in the right hand and repeat the pattern up the scale to end rhythmically with the 6th on *c″*.

(ii)   Repeat the right hand part and add bass 5ths to harmonise with the *second* of each ♪♪, making the first 6th of each pair a double appoggiatura. Although undecorated degrees 4–5 over chords IV–V produce displeasing parallel movement, you may hear that the zigzag melodic pattern caused by adding appoggiaturas makes the texture acceptable. The same applies to degrees 6–7 over chords IV–V (*SaK*, pp. 61–2) or you can use **HXB** to make a cadence at the top of the scale.

(iii)   Play a descending sequence in the same way, beginning:

Ex. 236

Use bass 5ths of V–I only, changing key with each bar. This time hear the first melody note of bar 2 also as degree 3, of a new key. Continue that process for two further bars, with a fifth-bar cadence to re-establish C major. Only in one case may the lower note of a 6th need inflecting to pass through the appropriate key. Although no new leading notes are played, they are implied, as you will find if you enrich the texture like this:

Ex. 237

Repertory Examples

These repertory examples are all developments of textures you have been using in this chapter. Investigate them and continue them or improvise in the same vein. Then, if you can, find the whole pieces quoted and compare your improvisations with the composition concerned.

(i)

Ex. 238 Harpsichord Sonata [Kirkpatrick 113]: opening   D. Scarlatti

Ex. 239 Ibid.: bars 30 - 33

(ii)

Ex. 240 Sonata, op. 2 no. 3: opening   L. van Beethoven

Landscape with one bass 5th per bar. Double the melody with 3rds or 6ths, as appropriate. Might there be one chromatic note?

(iii)

Ex. 241 **Sonata, op. 2 no. 3: opening of last movement**   *L. van Beethoven*

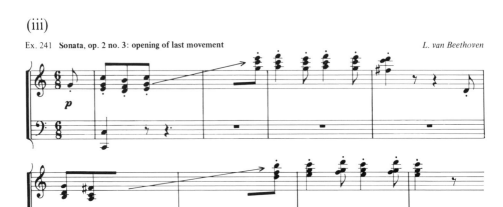

Supply the missing notes yourself.

(iv)

Ex. 242 **Piano Concerto in C, op. 15 no. 1: first movement bars 280 - 288**   *L. van Beethoven*

[Allegro con brio]

Notice the varied rhythmic arrangement of the $^6_3$s in successive phrases
and the change from parallel to contrary motion in the second half of
each phrase.

(v)

Ex. 243 **Sonata in A minor K.310: last movement, bars 38 - 40**   *W. A. Mozart*

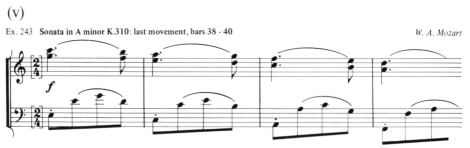

Here Mozart varies the $^6_3$ texture by wide leaps of registration.

(vi)

Ex. 244   Sonata in G, K.283: opening of last movement   W. A. *Mozart*

Mozart uses thirds above a tonic bass throughout this theme. Supply the missing notes and continue in the same style.

(vii)

Ex. 245   Sonata in A♭, op. 26: last movement   L. van *Beethoven*

This is what Beethoven made of the framework you used in Ex. 232. Notice again the inversion from the second half of bar 6.

(viii)

Ex. 246   Bagatelle in D, op. 33 no. 6: bars to the end   *L. van Beethoven*
   [Allegretto quasi Andante con una certa espressione parlante]

This coda uses 3rds and 6ths over a tonic pedal, most expressively.

(ix)

Ex. 247   **Valse Brillante in A♭, op. 34 no. 1: bars 17 – 32**   *F. Chopin*

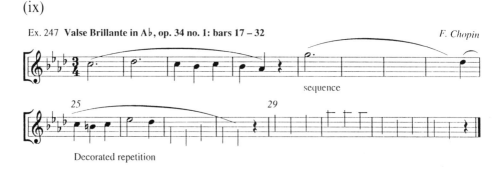

Decorated repetition

You will easily establish the harmonic framework of this passage by
landscaping in 5ths. Then double the melody in 3rds or 6ths and fit treble
and bass together. Then arrange bass note and upper chords for the left
hand in the texture commonly described as 'oom-pah-pah' and shown in
SaK, p. 252. Supply similar chromatic ornamentations in bars 29–32 to
those in bars 25–28. If you can see the published piece you will find it
easy to memorise, as you will remark and remember the differences from
your improvised treatment.

Folio

Add further pieces.

9   FILLING OUT

(*SaK 14, 15, 18*)

Some preliminary practice with the 3rds bass process ($\frac{}{3}$ in *SaK* shorthand, p. 188) will give you fluency for improvisation.

(i)   Re-play Ex. 199. Repeat the piece, transferring the lower right-hand line to the left hand as a $\frac{}{3}$ (a 10th below) and letting the right thumb take over the fifth of each chord:

Ex. 248

becomes

Ex. 249

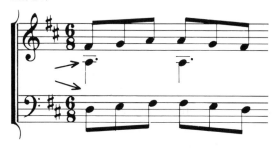

At each eight-bar cadence revert to right-hand 6ths over HXB. You can play the thumb-note once or twice in each bar *or* repeat it with each ♪ and play the whole texture staccato. In developing the piece as you did with $\frac{3}{5}$ you can make a variation by crossing the left hand over the right on repeated and subsequent bars.

(ii)   (a)   Play the first four bars of *This Old Man* (*SaK*, p. 30) on $\frac{}{3}$ harmonisation, then practise this short phrase in all keys, major and minor:

103

Ex. 250

[Repeat in dominant key]

Your fingers will soon find their way easily in any key. Concentrate on keeping the bass always a 3rd below the melody and do not double the bass notes in the right-hand part.

(b) Improvise a variation on this sequence, linking each repetition to that in the next key as shown:

Ex. 251

(c) Vary the passage again, by breaking up the right-hand chords into flowing triplets, beginning:

Ex. 252

(d) Another adaptation of broken-chord texture may begin with this right-hand pattern:

Ex. 253

Repertory Examples

Recognising the $\frac{}{3}$ origin of these repertory examples will help you to invent pieces of your own in similar styles and textures.

(i)

Ex. 254 Minuet K.1e   *W. A. Mozart*

Andante con moto

(ii)

Ex. 255 **Humming Song from 'Album for the Young', op.68 no. 3**   *R. Schumann*

(iii)

Ex. 256   Berceuse, op. 124 no. 6   R. Schumann

(iv)

Ex. 257   Prelude in G from 'The Well-Tempered Clavier' BWV 866   J. S. Bach

(This example is enhanced by the use of long tonic pedals.)

Ex. 258   Prelude in B♭ from 'The Well-Tempered Clavier', BWV 866   J. S. Bach

(v)

Ex. 259 Sonata in A, op. 2 no. 2: Trio opening in the Scherzo

L. van Beethoven

(Note the enrichment by contrary motion of the inner part in bars 2 and 4.)

(vi)

Ex. 260 Sonata in E minor, op. 90: second movement opening

L. van Beethoven

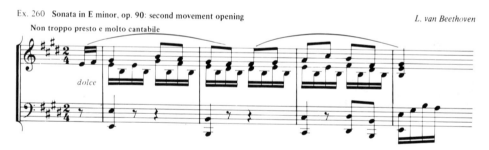

converted later to $\frac{}{3}$ over dominant pedal pivot notes:

(vii)

Ex. 261 Ibid.: bars 28 - 32

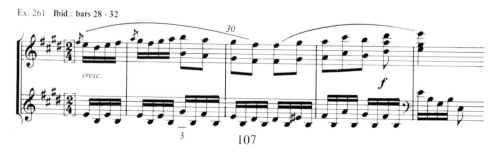

(viii)

R. Schumann

Add bar-lines to show which chords you would accent as first beats. It is important to realise that there is such a thing as 'harmonic rhythm' which establishes itself, irrespective of printed bar-lines. Compare your barring with that of a printed edition of this piece.

(See also Mozart Variation theme, *SaK*, p. 186.)

Starting Points

(i)   Add 3rds bass and continue in the style of Schumann:

Ex. 263

simile

(ii)   Improvise in the style of Bach:

Ex. 264

Then use the same pattern in C minor, in triple time.

(iii)

Ex. 265 **Minuet**

You may wish to use a thicker $\frac{}{3}$ texture here, but keep the little 'break' which fills in bar 2 light, in 3rds or 10ths. End the first eight bars with a nicely phrased imperfect cadence (*SaK*, p. 185, ex. 82). If you then repeat the opening phrase, strengthen the bass by dropping its register an octave, and end either with a perfect cadence in the tonic, or with a modulation to the dominant should you wish to continue the piece.

(iv)

Ex. 266 **Gavotte**

In the part of France where the inhabitants are called 'gavots', they also play a bagpipe called a 'musette'. When you have improvised a gavotte, largely on $\frac{}{3}$, add a musette in the relative minor on a tonic 5th drone. Relate the theme to that of the gavotte like this:

Ex. 267 **Musette**

(The acciaccatura is a pianist's attempt to imitate the bagpipe.)

(v)

Ex. 268

When the melody has ♩ ♪ you will only need a thumb-note as shown to keep the movement going. Fill in the final ♩ of the phrase with two right-hand triplets in 6ths to lead back to the tonic key. Vary the bass register as you proceed.

(vi) Play:

Ex. 269 **Song without Words, op. 85 no. 38**   *F. Mendelssohn*

(Note the ♩· appoggiaturas in bar 3)

In halved note-values, improvise a piece in the style of Mendelssohn:

Ex. 270

(vii)

Ex. 271 **Siciliano**

Try an extended passage near the end on 3rds or 6ths over a dominant Pedal, leading to a final cadence.

(viii)

Ex. 272 **Tarantella**

This improvisation in A minor should be in two parts, fast and light as befits a tarantella. The contrapuntal processes of chapter 2 are available as well as ⌐₃⌐, and the bass may occasionally take over ♪♪♪ or ♪ ♪ ; but over-elaboration will slow you down and lose the character of a tarantella.

(ix) Play Ex. 177 again, adding thumb-notes to produce a three-part texture. In the relative major section add a ♪ passing note at the end of the first left-hand bar.

(x)

Ex. 273

This is another piece needing a mixture of contrapuntal and harmonic thinking, as it involves a 3rds bass in mirror-image inversion, plus thumb-notes to complete the chords (*SaK*, pp. 203–204). Continue where the last bass ♪♪♪♪ leads.

111

(xi)

Ex. 274 **March**

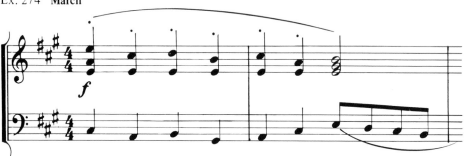

Notice the inverted $\overline{}_3$ in bar 2. As a minuet often had a contrasting three-part middle section called 'trio', so too do many marches. Add such a lighter section, with melody mainly in the rhythm 𝅗𝅥 ♩ ♩ .

(xii)

Ex. 275 **Waltz**

Use the texture practised in *SaK*, p. 227, with one bass ♩ to each bar.

(xiii) Play *Three Blind Mice* as a waltz, beginning:

Ex. 276 **Three Blind Mice Waltz**

Use $\overline{}_3$ where appropriate. In the phrase where the melody moves in ♩ ♩ ♩ thin the accompanying texture down to broken chord with the left hand.

Using All the Processes

Experiment in combining all the processes in this book by improvising the exposition section of a classical sonata movement in the style of Mozart or Beethoven, on this framework. Use a major or minor key.

First subject: Improvise a theme doubled at the octave (in any registration).

Bridge Passage: Choose any of the 'passage-work' textures and modulate to a related key relevant to your choice of major or minor first subject.

Second subject: Improvise a melody with accompaniment in the new key, contrasted with the first subject. The accompaniment might precede the entry of the melody and you might use the two-note pattern, or $\frac{}{3}$ in a flowing texture, or any other process not yet used in the piece.

Codetta: Improvise an extended decorated cadence firmly establishing the key of the second subject. Close or extended broken chords, ornaments and varied registration may be useful here.

For repertory examples look at any Mozart or Beethoven sonatas which announce the first theme in octaves, and Mozart's 'Sonata Facile', K. 545 for textures of the other sections.

Folio

You may well need to write down this ambitious improvisation by sections to remember it. When you have it safely in your folio, improvise further expositions.

10 ALL ON A PAR

(SaK 17)

In the carol *Unto us a boy is born* (*SaK*, p. 195) two new harmonic idioms were added to the vocabulary, both useful for improvisation: the use of chord V_c^7 to avoid objectionable parallels when chords IV–V are needed under a rising melody (*SaK*, p. 196, last paragraph); and secondly, the bass sequence of descending 5ths (*SaK*, p. 199). To gain fluency in their use, play two exercises with variations:

(i) (a) Play this two-bar passage through all keys. The last melody note of each phrase becomes the 5th degree of the next key, the subdominant. For the second of each pair of keys, drop the register of the melody instead of rising in the second bar, so that you stay in the middle area of the keyboard.

Ex. 277

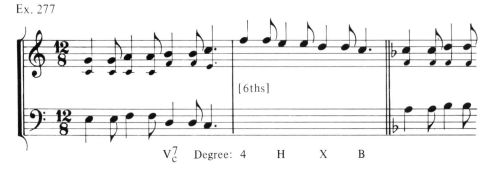

(b) Play the same sequence on these right-hand rhythmic patterns, which you used in the last chapter:

Ex. 278

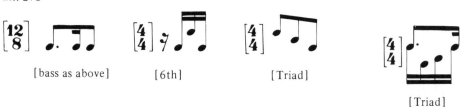

In the last pattern, bar 2 may now be varied by extraneous passing notes like this:

Ex. 279

(ii)

(a) A similar zigzag melodic line in bar 5 of *Unto us a boy is born* provides the basis for this sequence, but with a different chord for each note. Continue the sequence all the way down the scale to end with a V–I cadence (nine *pairs of chords*):

Ex. 280 (a)   (b)

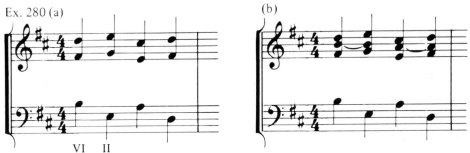

VI   II

(b) Improvise on this sequence using these patterns (and any others you can devise):

Ex. 281
Allegro

Ex. 282
Andante

Ex. 283
Allegretto

Ex. 284

(c)   First *sing* this last variation in descending sequence, while you divide the accompaniment between your hands, left thumb and little finger maintaining the bass progression. Then *play* the melody, with the left hand jumping between bass note and chord. When you play what you sang you may find that you had instinctively made occasional chromatic alterations to the lower note of the turn on the second beat—a case where ear and voice may do better than fingers!

Ex. 285

Early eighteenth century composers of the Baroque period used this sequence extensively:

Ex. 286   Concerto Grosso in D minor, op. 3 no. 11: bars 51 - 54   *A. Vivaldi*

Ex. 286a   Ibid.: bars 43 - 47

116

Starting Points

The full-chord version of Ex. 280(b) can have any one of the three notes at the top. If you put the tied note at the top, you will play:

Ex. 287

(i)   Use this pattern:

Ex. 288

[Two-bar sequence, 3rd lower]

(ii)   Now play these ♩s in Ex. 287 below the 3rds and replace the original circle of fifths in the bass; then continue the sequence.

Ex. 289

Develop this starting point which derives from it:

Ex. 290
Gravely

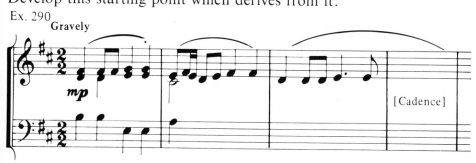

mp

[Cadence]

This enriched texture of $^6_4$ s over the bass sequence in octaves raises the dynamic level and may be used as a climax to the piece:

Ex. 291

(Note the *triple* appoggiatura on the third beat.) When you reach a diminished chord, either modify it or skip that pair of chords.

Modulating with the Circle of Fifths

The circle of fifths can be used to modulate into keys on various degrees of any scale.

(i)   Play the sequence all the way down the scale, as in Ex. 280, beginning:

Ex. 292

(ii)   Re-play the first two bars. Then play them again, altering the g' in bar 2 to g#'. This raised note leads you to the relative minor key. Follow these two bars with another to confirm a cadence in the new key.

(iii) Re-play the original first two bars (with g♮') and continue the sequence, this time raising the first melody note of bar 3. Where does this lead you?

(iv)   Return to the first two bars and find out what chromatic alteration is necessary to reach the subdominant key by the end of bar 3. (The melody does not change.)

(v)   Now descend the unaltered sequence in C again, until you can modulate to the key on the third degree (E minor) by raising the 6th needed to form its leading note. Because it is the relative minor of the dominant key, G major, you will need to raise both notes of the 6th. Add an HXB cadence to establish the new key.

(vi)   Lastly, descend the tonal sequence still further until you can modulate to the key on the 2nd degree (D minor) by producing its leading note in the relevant 6th. As D minor is the relative minor of the subdominant key, F major, you may find the first necessary accidental is a B flat, somewhere in either or both hands. Try out the various possibilities.

You will now be able to use the 'circle of fifths' under right-hand 6ths to modulate to keys on the first six degrees of *any* scale (all the 'related' keys). You can do this in any of the patterns of examples 281–5.

Counterpoint on the Circle of Fifths

(i)

Ex. 293

Continue this pattern in descending sequence.

(ii)   Repeat the melodic line of Ex. 293 with the bass elaborated to this pattern in each bar:

Ex. 294

This will slow down the tempo, as you treat each chord in terms of the 3-note motif of chapter 2 in the bass. Combining harmonic terminology with that of counterpoint, this pattern can now be described as an alternation between root and first inversion of the chord concerned; the *harmony* unfolds in *linear* fashion, as is so often the case.

(iii)

Ex. 295

Continue this pattern in ascending sequence.

Starting Points

Now that you can use chords on all degrees of the scale, you will find that a double unit of the 3-note motif, applied to such a *pair of chords*, is open to all sorts of variants. The important thing is to think first of *ideas*, such as ascend, descend, invert, double or treble the speed of one part in relation to the other, change bar-time and vary rhythmic patterns. Then, after you have used your imagination, turn the ideas into notes. This is the motif and its inversion:

Ex. 296

(i)   This might be your initial use of that two-chord contrapuntal unit for a sequential area of a piece:

Ex. 297

(ii) *Idea*   Exchange parts:

Ex. 298

(iii) *Idea*   Reverse motif:

Ex. 299

(iv) *Idea*   Exchange parts again:

Ex. 300

(v) *Idea*   Change rhythmic pattern and thicken texture:

Ex. 301

(vi) *Idea*   Exchange parts and lighten texture:

Ex. 302

(vii) Harmonic sequences, with all chords 'on a par', produce music essentially in transit—material for bridge passages or development sections. Firm cadences are needed from time to time to provide the anchorage of a new or former key. Improvise a piece on this starting point in the style of Bach:

Ex. 303

including a sequential passage beginning:

Ex. 304

Continue to a cadence in the relative major, then use another sequential passage to modulate to another cadence in the home key, perhaps beginning:

Ex. 305

Continue with four or more bars of your initial theme transposed into F major and repeated in D minor. Leap an octave in the melody and find your way back to A minor for your final section.

(viii) Such contrapuntal passages based on circle of fifths harmony can be used to reach a climax in a development section:

Ex. 306

The sense of climax is increased if you raise the first note of each bar by a semitone, suggesting passing modulations:

Ex. 307

You may hear the bass line *either* as a melodic counterpoint *or* as the roots of two chords (V and I). Such strong bass roots have a sedentary effect. To make a smoother, more mobile bass use the two-note accompaniment pattern of page 52 to express the harmonies of V-I. This pattern too was conceived melodically, as degrees 4-5, 3-5 of the scale. Whether you think contrapuntally of the two halves of the scale:

Ex. 308

or think in vertical harmonic terms of:

Ex. 309

V^7_d I_b

a one-bar pattern based on this idea will provide fine scope for a more interesting contrapuntal climax. You only need to think consciously that the first notes in each hand are degrees '4' and '7' of each key's scale: the rest will follow naturally:

Ex. 310

(ix) Build a similar climax on this variant:

Ex. 311

più cresc.

(x) This may lower the tension:

Ex. 312

dim. [Cadence in G minor]

(xi) Improvise a piece on the framework of a complete sonata movement, starting with an exposition as outlined at the end of the previous chapter (page 113). After that exposition, invent a development section making use of the contrapuntal ideas you have used here. Add a recapitulation, based on the exposition without modulation, and end with a coda, which might include a dominant or tonic Pedal bass.

Folio

Inclusion of this complete sonata movement, based on the varied musical vocabulary and textures you have been learning to improvise will provide encouraging evidence of your progress and convince you that you *can* make your own music. Once you have broken the barrier of believing improvisation to be out of your reach, it will become an enjoyable pursuit of ever increasing discovery for a lifetime.